Edited by
Wayne Rice

HELP!
THERE'S A TEENAGER
IN MY HOUSE

A Troubleshooting Guide for Parents

IVP

InterVarsity Press
Downers Grove, Illinois

InterVarsity Press
P.O. Box 1400, Downers Grove, IL 60515-1426
World Wide Web: www.ivpress.com
E-mail: mail@ivpress.com

InterVarsity Press® is the book-publishing division of InterVarsity Christian Fellowship/USA®, a student movement active on campus at hundreds of universities, colleges and schools of nursing in the United States of America, and a member movement of the International Fellowship of Evangelical Students. For information about local and regional activities, write Public Relations Dept., InterVarsity Christian Fellowship/USA, 6400 Schroeder Rd., P.O. Box 7895, Madison, WI 53707-7895, or visit the IVCF website at <www.intervarsity.org>.

All Scripture quotations, unless otherwise indicated, are taken from the Holy Bible, New International Version®. NIV®. Copyright ©1973, 1978, 1984 by International Bible Society. Used by permission of Zondervan Publishing House. All rights reserved.

Design: Cindy Kiple

Images: man with contorted face: Tim Platt/Getty Images
        girl jumping: Mark Andersen/Getty Images
        teenager surfing: SW Productions/Getty Images
        all other images: Rubberball Productions/Getty Images

ISBN 0-8308-3286-6
Printed in the United States of America ∞

Library of Congress Cataloging-in-Publication Data

Help! There's a teenager in my house: a troubleshooting guide for
parents / Wayne Rice, editor.
    p. cm.
 ISBN 0-8308-3286-6 (pbk.: alk. paper)
 1. Parenting—Religious aspects—Christianity. 2. Christian
teenagers—Religious life. 3. Parent and teenager—Religious
aspects—Christianity. I. Rice, Wayne.
  BV4529.H45 2005
  248.8'45—dc22

2005004487

P	19	18	17	16	15	14	13	12	11	10	9	8	7	6	5	4	3	2	1
Y	19	18	17	16	15	14	13	12	11	10	09	08	07	06	05					

To all the great parents who have attended our

Understanding Your Teenager seminars over the years.

We have learned much from you!

CONTENTS

3 COMMUNICATION

4 DATING AND SEXUALITY

INTRODUCTION

Adolescence can be baffling at times.

Maybe you're a parent who

- wonders why your fourteen-year-old daughter seems oblivious to the pile of toxic waste that now occupies most of her bedroom floor

- has a fifteen-year-old son who can score twenty billion points on any computer game in existence but is totally clueless about how to use the controls on a vacuum cleaner

- can't understand why your sixteen-year-old daughter yells, "You're the worst mother in the history of the world!" one minute and then, "Mom, can you help me with my homework?" the next

- wonders why your once-charming little kid has suddenly become the poster boy for aggressive, disruptive, oppositional, defiant disorder

- can't figure out why your daughter can volunteer for every school activity and run the political campaigns for all her friends with ability, enthusiasm and success . . . but is overwhelmed by a simple request to do the dishes

- can't understand why your fifteen-year-old son gets up and walks out of the room every time you walk into it

Well, you'll be glad to know that most of these parents (along with their kids) are normal. You are not alone. And no matter how baffling adolescent behavior might seem to you, there are answers to most of the questions you have about how to be a good parent. That's why we wrote this book—we want to encourage you and provide you with the help you need.

This book answers 101 of the most common questions we have received from parents who have attended our Understanding Your Teenager seminars and from parents who have sought help from our website (www.uyt.com). Organized by topic, these questions have answers written by 9 members of our seminar team, who together have more than 250 years of experience working with teenagers and who have been parents of teenagers themselves.

And while each of the writers answer the questions in this book from his or her own unique experience and perspective, there are common threads that you will notice throughout the book.

The first thread is a shared faith in Jesus Christ. Each question is answered in light of Scripture, recognizing that the Bible doesn't always speak directly to every situation we face in today's world. Adolescence didn't exist as a stage of life when the Bible was written. But we have answered each question with the understanding that the Bible does provide for us the principles we need to respond to every situation in a biblical and Christlike way.

The second thread is a shared view of adolescence. Because we are all youth workers, we like and enjoy being around teenagers. It's unfortunate that so many psychologists view adolescence as a time of inevitable trouble—perhaps because they spend most of their time with troubled kids. We have a more positive view—perhaps because we spend a lot of time with "good kids" as well as those who are having problems. In fact, we believe that most kids can become good kids if they get enough encouragement and guidance from adults who care about them, especially parents.

Another common thread is a shared understanding of particular parenting principles and concepts that we affirm and teach at our Understanding Your Teenager seminars. Here are a few of them:

- Today's teenagers are growing up in a different world. They face challenges that are unique to their generation, and as parents we must respond creatively and appropriately to those challenges.

- Teenagers are in transition. They are leaving behind their childhood and becoming adults.

- Teenagers are seeking autonomy. They are separating from their parents in order to establish identities of their own.

- Teenagers are expanding their relationships. While children seek playmates, teenagers seek close friends and mentors outside the home.

- Teenagers are equipping themselves for adulthood. Adolescence is a time for learning the life skills that will help them become capable, self-reliant adults.

- Teenagers are developing personal values and beliefs. It's normal for teens to challenge everything they have been taught in order to arrive at a value system and faith that will sustain them for the rest of their lives.

- Parents are not only the most powerful influence but also the most enduring influence on teenagers.

- The better the relationship parents have with their teenager, the more likely that teenager will respect their authority.

- Teens respond better to encouragement than criticism. Catch your teenager in the act of doing something good.

- Not every issue or behavior is worth fighting over. Pick your battles wisely or you'll be battling all the time.

- Parents help their teenagers learn right from wrong by talking to them, spending time with them and being an example for them.

- Parents help their teenagers become responsible and self-reliant by not overindulging them and by allowing them to learn from their experiences.

- The best way to discipline a teenager is by consistently connecting his or her behavior with natural or logical consequences.

- There is no such thing as a perfect parent, but every parent can be a successful parent by doing what he or she knows is the right thing to do.

These principles may sound like common sense (which they are), but common sense doesn't come to mind when your teenager has just proclaimed you to be the dumbest parent in the history of the world. One of our goals is to remind you that parenting is not rocket science. You probably already know what you need to know. You can do it. But it's easy to become distracted and overwhelmed by the challenges of parenting teenagers in today's world. We want to help you refocus and remember that for every problem, there's a solution not far away.

You may want to sit down and read this book all the way through, even though the questions and answers might not seem to apply to you. By reading the entire book, you'll be prepared for potential problems, plus you'll have some information you can use to help others. If the questions (or answers) seem repetitious, that's not entirely by accident. We hope that by repeating ourselves, we can impress on you the truth of the principles we are trying to apply.

On the other hand, you may want to use this book mainly as a reference—only looking up questions and answers when you need them. That's okay too. Just don't forget it's up there on your bookshelf!

Keep in mind that while the questions in this book are real questions asked by real parents, they are only "examples" of questions that parents commonly ask. Your questions undoubtedly will be different. You live in a different place, your family is different, your kids are different, and most importantly, *you* are different. For that reason, you'll need to be both flexible and a bit skeptical. It's okay to disagree with us. Frankly, we don't always agree with each other! Besides, we don't know the whole story behind your situation, which might actually result in a completely different answer than the one that is given. We offer our answers also as "examples" from which you can learn some larger principles and make your own application. We can't tell you what to do—only you can decide that.

Many of the questions in this book specify age, but not all. Some of them refer simply to "my teenager," "my son" or "my daughter." Keep in mind that most of our answers will need to be applied quite differently for a thirteen-year-old than an eighteen-year-old. Not every answer makes this distinction, so you will have to use your best judgment depending on the age and maturity of your teenager. (Hint: it's appropriate to impose all kinds of limits and controls on a thirteen-year-old's behavior; it's not for an eighteen-year-old.)

We want this book to be a big help to you, but we don't want it to be a substitute for getting professional help. If you are at the end of your rope, don't expect any book (including this one) to provide you with something that only an experienced counselor can provide. If you or your teenager are in danger, contact someone who can help right away. Below are some questions to think about. If you answer yes to any of them, your teenager needs assessment and professional help as soon as possible.

- Is your teen involved in any kind of drug abuse?
- Does your teen have an eating disorder? Is your teen obsessed with diet and exercise?
- Does your teen engage in self-mutilation? Any homemade tattoos or "cutting"?
- Has your teen suddenly dropped out of school?
- Is your home life in chaos because of your teen?
- Is your teenager involved in the occult?
- Does your teenager have a serious anger-management problem? Does he or she get into fights a lot?
- Does your teenager talk about death a lot? Any threats of suicide?
- Does your teenager seem unusually depressed?
- Does your teenager have a sleep disorder (either sleeping too little or too much)?
- Does your teen seem fearful of another family member? Could there be a chance of sexual or physical abuse that your teen doesn't want to talk about?
- Does your teen abuse alcohol?
- Has your teenager recently dumped all his or her old friends for new ones? Does the new group seem antisocial or ganglike?
- Do you and your teen experience constant conflict or an inability to communicate without yelling, foul language or physical violence?

That list is not comprehensive, of course. There are other good reasons to seek counsel, intervention or therapy, and we trust that you will always be willing to get your teenager the help that he or she needs. Get help for yourself, too, if you need it. Your personal well-being and your behavior will have a tremendous impact on your teenager and your ability to be an effective parent. When you get those emergency instructions on a jet plane, you are always reminded to put on your oxygen mask first and then to help your child or someone else if necessary. That's good advice for parents as well as passengers. Changing yourself is always more important than changing your teenager. The better you are, the better your kids will be.

Parenting teenagers today can definitely be a challenge, but we believe that most kids still want to have a good relationship with their parents and want parents who aren't afraid to set limits and provide guidance for them. Teenagers don't want to live in a home without rules. They may want fewer or more reasonable rules, but never no rules. So don't give up. Trust that your kids are capable of growing into mature, self-reliant and responsible adults. It's the job of parents to encourage them and to help them become the young men and women that God created them to be. We hope this book will help you to do just that.

Wayne Rice
Founder, Understanding Your Teenager Seminars

FAMILY AND HOME LIFE

1. Our fifteen-year-old daughter's bedroom is a disaster area. We have asked her repeatedly to clean her room at least once a week, but she insists that it's her room and she has a right to keep it a mess if she wants to. We know we shouldn't fight battles over insignificant issues, but she doesn't have that many responsibilities around the house. Is keeping her bedroom clean too much to ask? What do you think?

You are correct that failure to keep a clean bedroom doesn't rank high on our list of problem teen behaviors. Still, you do have the right to expect your daughter to maintain her living quarters up to the housekeeping standards that you have established for your home. Next time she asserts that the room is hers, you might remind her that you are the one who pays the mortgage, lights, fire insurance, heating and air conditioning, and so forth. The room is on loan to her until the day when she is emancipated, at which time it reverts back to you and gets turned into an office. Meanwhile, she is responsible to take care of this space and make sure it comes back to you in good condition.

There's no need to engage in a power struggle over this issue; this is not the hill you want to die on. There is, however, a tried-and-tested strategy used by some parents that may solve the problem without serious conflict. Simply tell your daughter that if she doesn't keep her room clean according to the standards that you have set (be specific and reasonable about those standards), then you will be happy to do it for her. If the room is not clean on the particular day of the week that you have mutually agreed on, then you'll gladly go into her bedroom and put everything in order, including her dresser drawers, the shelves in her closet, her cabinets, desk drawers and any other place where she might store personal items. The room will then be clean and you will be happy. You might even charge a small fee for this service, which can be deducted from her allowance.

Don't worry. You won't have to do this more than once. What you are doing is forcing your daughter to choose which is most important to her: privacy or a messy room. If your daughter is normal (and it sounds like she is), she'll choose privacy by a landslide.

Wayne Rice

2. *We believe that it's important for our sons to be responsible, so we've assigned them a few household chores. For example, we've asked our thirteen-year-old to make sure our trash and recyclables are ready for pick-up once a week. Our fifteen-year-old has to mow the lawn. But so far, they've done nothing but gripe. We really don't know how to motivate them or punish them for their refusal to do chores. We don't want to let them off the hook, but we really don't want chores to become a serious source of conflict between us. Any suggestions?*

Make a list of all the chores that need to get done around the house, including the ones that you do. Determine how much time each chore takes and record it in writing. Most families have over twenty hours of work per week just to keep things going. Make sure you include washing clothes, folding them and putting them away, and all the time that goes into food: planning a menu, making the grocery list, shopping, shelving, organizing, cooking, cleaning up after the meal and so on. This will help your teens see that there is much to do and that everyone needs to do their part for things to be fair. Then assign a name to each task (of course, as parents you will have more hours assigned in addition to your day jobs, so it won't be even).

Emphasize to your sons that everyone needs to contribute to the team—Team Family. Families have members, not guests, so they can't afford to have spectators; we all need to contribute. You could ask your teens, "What happens if I stop doing the laundry or grocery shopping?" "What might happen if Dad doesn't feel like working and doesn't go to the office?" Part of life is learning to do what we'd rather not do. It's not easy, it's not always fun, but being mature means doing the right thing even when we don't feel like it. It's putting our self-discipline ahead of our feelings.

When everyone does his task without being nagged to do it, home life is much smoother. If one of your sons refuses to do his job, assign him another one. Say, "You have just earned an additional job. This is because I have to take time to talk to you about this—time that could be spent doing my share of the tasks. Instead, I'm talking to you about your contribution. You owe me thirty minutes of extra chores, plus you need to finish your regular duty before you go out tonight. If you gripe about it, I'll add another thirty minutes of work—your choice."

Make sure that you affirm your sons for the work they do as a contribution to the family. Don't be too picky about how thorough it is at first; just applaud any progress in the right direction. They will be more likely to do a better job and to finish it in the future if you express appreciation for their efforts. Don't expect perfection, but affirm progress.

Tim Smith

3. We have a twenty-year-old living at home, and we are having a great deal of conflict with him. We know that we can't treat him like a child anymore, but we have rules that we expect him to obey as long as he is still living in our house. His younger brothers and sisters don't understand why he gets to do things they are not allowed to do. Are we wrong to demand that he respect our rules?

No, you are not. After all, it's your house, and as long as your son lives at home, he needs to realize that there are going to be house rules that you have determined are important and must be enforced. These rules may include such issues as acceptable behavior in the house (e.g., no smoking, no alcohol, no loud music, etc.), finances (who pays for what), responsibilities (chores) and so on. This is something anyone would expect if they were living in someone else's house. Once he has a place of his own, he can make up his own set of house rules.

You can't really control him at the age of twenty, however. At our Understanding Your Teenager seminars, we teach that there are five stages of parenting. They are:

- Stage One: Catering (0-2 years). You do everything for the child.

- Stage Two: Controlling (2-10 years). You micromanage the child's life.

- Stage Three: Coaching (10-14 years). You let your child start making more of his or her own choices.

- Stage Four: Consulting (14-18 years). You allow your teenager to make most of his or her own choices.

- Stage Five: Caring (18+). You're done.

At age twenty your son is in that last stage, which takes you completely out of the control loop. Do you care what happens to your son? Of course you do, but it's all up to him. You have to allow your son to take responsibility for his own life. You can't make demands on him beyond those that directly affect you or others in your family.

You can still set limits for your other teenagers that are appropriate for their age and individual needs. These are not negated by your older son's noncompliance to them. It's helpful for kids to see that as they get older, their freedom increases. When they are twenty, they too will be able to make their own decisions regarding such things as curfew, church attendance, how they spend money and the like. In fact, sometimes younger kids can learn a lot from the dumb mistakes of their older siblings and avoid repeating them.

If your twenty-year-old is living at home and depending on you for support, then it's not unreasonable to expect certain things from him in return. If you are paying tuition for college, then he must maintain his grades. If you are providing room and board, then he should either pay rent or help with household chores. Rules like these have nothing to do with your being a parent. They have more to do with your natural need to not let anyone take advantage of you or your generosity.

HOME SWEET HOME

When an older son or daughter is unhappy with the rules of the home, it's very helpful for them to get an apartment of their own. The hassles of living at home will no longer be an issue.

I used to complain a lot about the rules and expectations of my parents when I was a nineteen-year-old living at home. So I moved out and rented an apartment. I couldn't believe that they charged me not only for rent but for gas and electric, phone, water, trash disposal and insurance. It didn't take long for me to realize that I didn't have it so bad at home after all. After I moved out there were no more home-cooked meals, no one to do my laundry, wash the dishes and keep the place clean! Hey Mom and Dad, can I have my room back?

Jim Green

It's not easy to let go or to allow your kids to do things you don't approve of, but at some point kids need to learn the hard way that they are in control of their own lives. If they are still living in your house, the rules that you have in place can help them on this journey, along with reasonable and respectful consequences when they choose not to abide by them.

Wayne Rice

4. *Since our children were little, we've used our vacation time to visit relatives we rarely get to see. We believe that it's important for our children to know their extended family. But this year our kids are complaining about our vacation plans. They want to do something different. Do you have any suggestions on how we can make our family vacation more appealing to our teenagers and still visit relatives?*

As children get older, their interests change, and they want to put anything that they consider childish behind them. Teenagers are moving toward independence, so they push for separation from mom and dad and family traditions, even treasured ones. All this is normal.

Next time you discuss vacation plans with your kids, begin by acknowledging their requests, letting them know that you empathize with them and understand their point of view. Then explain to them (without nagging, yelling, threatening or getting emotional) why you believe family traditions and visiting extended family members are important. Then ask for their suggestions for a compromise solution. They may come up with some reasonable ideas. For example, they may suggest that you take another vacation in addition to the trip to visit the relatives. Or while you're on the way to visiting relatives, you could do something fun like go to a nearby amusement park or beach. Make a few suggestions of your own. You could suggest that they invite a friend to go along, or you could promise to let them have their own room when you stay at a hotel. It may cost you a little more money, but it's usually worth it to have happy campers.

Your teenagers may still be bugged that they have to visit Grandma, Grandpa and Aunt Mabel—but they'll appreciate your efforts to see things from their point of view and to arrive at a good solution.

Dave Veerman

5. **We have some rules for our kids, but they seem to ignore them a good deal of the time. When we remind them of the rules, they plead ignorance, or say they misunderstood the rules. We are thinking of writing them down into a kind of family constitution. Do you think this is a good idea?**

Yes, I think it's a great idea, and while you're at it, you can work in a history lesson! Imagine our country without a Constitution; we'd be all over the map. But for over two hundred years we have been able to follow the guidelines of our country's founders and fulfill their vision of a nation "for the people and by the people" that allows individuals to pursue life, liberty and happiness. Our Constitution gives us a framework to live and make decisions by. Families would benefit from a family constitution in the same way.

We have done an excellent job of affirming individual rights and expression of those rights in our country, but we have not done as good a job with helping our kids understand the benefits and responsibilities of community. Many teens believe the world revolves around them. It doesn't, of course, and the sooner they learn this, the better off they'll be. Individual rights are important, but we need to help our teens understand that they have a role and a responsibility to the community—beginning with their family.

Schedule a family meeting and announce that you are going to work together to develop a constitution to guide your family, something that will help each family member remember what's important and to think "community" instead of "me first." Ask them, "What are the core values that we should have as part of our family constitution? What are the important ideas that we want to see present in how we relate to each other and in the decisions we make?" If you are getting resistance from your teens over this idea, let them know, "This is your opportunity to make this family different, but you have to express your opinion and share your ideas."

Record the ideas in writing and then say, "Let's think about these for a week, then we will get back together to affirm or edit these concepts." At the next session, try to come up with three or four key concepts that can represent your top family values. For instance, you could take three themes from our forefathers: life, liberty and the pursuit of happiness. "Life" could be the essentials of living together. "Liberty" could be the freedom to pursue our individual interests and have our own life. And the "pursuit of happiness" could refer to the things we can do to bring joy to each other and to those outside of the family.

Once you have decided on your key concepts, make a chart like the one below. In the first column, record these key values; in the second column, record the behavior that reflects these values (the rules); and in the third column, describe the consequences—positive and negative—that will happen to family members who follow or don't follow the preferred behavior. This approach helps teens own the rules because they were involved in making them, and it helps them understand the *why* behind the rules. It also helps you because an act of misbehavior has a negative consequence that has been agreed on in advance. This way you avoid the last-minute anxiety of "What should I do to punish him this time?"

Top Family Values	Desired Behavior	Consequences (+ & -)
Life	To be responsible and respectful with common family possessions	Enjoy the use of family possessions (TV, DVD player, etc.) or lose them for a week
Liberty	To have time alone, personal space and personal possessions	Enjoy privacy or lose privacy (door must remain open)
Pursuit of happiness	To spend time with family at dinner, outings, church activities, etc.	Enjoy time together or lose time with friends on weekends

Tim Smith

6. **What about curfew? We don't allow our fifteen-year-old to stay out past eleven o'clock, but lately she's been complaining that we're unfair and old-fashioned. All her friends get to stay out later, she says, and she doesn't understand why she has to come home so early. She thinks we don't trust her and that we're treating her like a child. We just don't want to worry about her safety. Are we being unreasonable to expect her home at a decent hour?**

Curfew rules come in many different varieties, but they are usually necessary as your teenagers are gaining more and more freedom. You don't want to worry about your kids when they are out with their friends. Setting limits on how long teenagers can keep you worrying is not old-fashioned or unfair. It's a perfectly reasonable thing for parents to do.

However, for most teenagers, curfews are viewed as a challenge to their freedom. As long as they exist, your teens will try to test your resolve to enforce them. In our home, we told our daughters that they didn't have a curfew—we just wanted to know where they were going, who they were with and what they were doing every time they went out. That way they had to negotiate with us how late they could stay out. This allowed for more flexibility for weekdays, weekends, special occasions and activities. Different situations often require different rules. I think we gained more information this way than if we had a "be home by 11:00" rule. On school nights, they were expected to be home by 9 p.m. unless there was some valid reason to be out later.

You probably have experienced the response "I dunno, just hangin' out" when you asked your teen what she is planning on doing. In some cases, it's okay to let things develop, if you trust her and the people she is hanging out with. If you are doubtful, get more information. With the advent of cell phones, plans can change and your teen's social agenda can turn on a dime. Make sure they use the phone to call you and keep you posted of any changes. The basic rule is "No surprises." Let them know, "I don't want to be surprised to find out who you were with, what you were doing or where you were. It's to your advantage to keep me informed or your world will become very small."

> **PUTTING OUT FIRES**
>
> The word curfew comes from an ancient word meaning "to put out the fire." If our forefathers waited too late to extinguish a fire, it could flame up and burn down the whole village during the night. So they had a curfew—a time to put out the fire.
>
> Perhaps the word's meaning still holds true for today's teenagers.
>
> Jim Green

This approach shows trust, enhances parent-teen dialogue and develops negotiating skills. I think teens like to announce to their friends, "I don't have a curfew. I just talked to my dad and told him I'd be home around 11:30. He was cool with that."

One reason why we went with this "floating curfew" idea is that curfews don't necessarily result in good behavior. Parents sometime falsely reason, *If she's home in time, she's not getting into trouble,* and they don't bother to get enough information. Teens can still get in trouble and make it home by curfew. With the floating curfew your teen may need to come home one hour after the football game ends, instead of a specific time. That gives her time to chat with friends, get pizza and get home. It also allows you as the parent to be flexible when the situation warrants it, like out-of-town games, formals and proms, and concerts.

You might try this approach with your daughter. Sometimes the chance to stay out later reduces the resentment of being told when to come in, but it also forces her to be responsible to dialogue with you and negotiate an acceptable time to be home.

Tim Smith

7. *What should we do if our teenager doesn't obey the rules completely? For example, if curfew is 11:00, what if he comes home at 11:10? Should we make him suffer for ten minutes? Should we overlook small infractions or be tough? We don't want to be taken advantage of.*

This is the perfect time to teach logical consequences. Be calm and firm ("tough") when you explain that coming home ten minutes after curfew this night means that he will have to come home ten minutes earlier the next night (that's not suffering too much!). Don't allow the discussion to be about you and your rules. Keep the focus on your son's behavior and choices. You could say, for example, "I'm sorry that you chose to come home late. As you know, this means that to-morrow's curfew is ten minutes earlier. Hopefully that will help you remember to leave when you need to so that you can get home on time." If you want to motivate your teenager a little more, you can adjust the consequence accordingly. For example, "If you come home ten minutes late, you'll be required to come home twenty minutes earlier next time you go out."

Just be clear on your rules and enforce them consistently—otherwise they won't work for you very well. For example, when you say, "Be home at 11:00 p.m.," specify exactly what that means: "Every part of you must be in the house with the door closed behind you before the clock on the microwave oven (not your watch, my watch or the clock in the car) reads 11:00 p.m. If you discover that you can't make it home by that time, call me immediately and we'll talk it over and decide what to do."

Remember—the clearer you are on the rules and the consequences, the easier it will be to decide how to handle infractions. And of course it's always a good idea to remember the principle *Choose your battles wisely.*

Dave Veerman

8. *We have rules for our children, and we have been quite firm in enforcing them. But our kids argue that some of those rules are dumb and should be changed. We aren't so sure. If we change one rule, then all the rules are up for grabs. What do you think?*

Most rules aren't set in concrete. As your kids get older, some of them will need to be changed or eliminated entirely. (You can probably lose that rule you have about throwing your baby bottle on the floor.)

Some rules, however, are "house rules" that never change: clean up after yourself, be considerate of others and respectful to their property and so on. These are essential rules for families or anyone who lives together. It is helpful to separate rules into two lists—one for developing the character of the teen and one for general house rules.

With the personal character rules, the idea is to focus on what you see is an area of character development for the teen. For instance, your thirteen-year-old son may be somewhat lazy about taking regular showers and keeping up on his personal hygiene. You wouldn't want a house rule that everyone must have a daily shower! But for him, you could have a discussion that lets him know this is important and it is one of the three things you are going to be working on with him in the next few months. By focusing on three areas (rather than dozens), you don't overwhelm your teen or become too critical. It also keeps you from becoming stressed due to battling over too many issues.

I also recommend that you narrow your house rules to a short list and post them where family members can see them. One family I know has reduced it to one phrase: "I can do anything I want as long as I consider the needs of others and act accordingly."

When it comes to dealing with the accusations that your rules are dumb, let them know the *why* behind the rule. Then challenge them, "If you can think of another way to reinforce this value, let me know; until then, you need to follow my dumb rule because I am trying to help you learn this

CHANGING CURFEW RULES

Ask your teenager, "How would you like to have no curfew at all?" Most teens will be very interested in that concept.

Here's how to do it: Set a reasonable curfew for them when they are young—say 10:00 p.m. for age fourteen. Then, when they reach fourteen and a half, extend it to 10:30. At age fifteen, make it 11:00. At age fifteen and a half, 11:30. By age sixteen, midnight. At age sixteen and a half—no curfew at all. All they have to do is tell you when they expect to be home, and unless there's a good reason why the time they request is unreasonable, you will permit them to stay out.

But here's the catch. They can't break curfew at any of the other stages along the way; otherwise, curfew will be extended for an additional six-month period. Be reasonable, of course, and define what it means to "break" curfew. If your teenager tried and failed, let him or her learn from their mistake with an appropriate consequence. You might want to include a "grace period" to allow for honest mistakes. But if your teen violates your trust with disobedience, they need to know that they lose their right to early freedom.

The principle here is simple: trust must be earned. If teenagers prove themselves trustworthy, then there's no reason to believe they can't be trusted to eventually govern their own behavior. They'll be doing that someday whether you like it or not.

Wayne Rice

important principle." One word of warning: never argue with your teenager about the rules. Save your breath. Until they are a parent themselves, they'll never see things from your point of view. Just decide which rules are important for your kids, and enforce them without second-guessing yourself or getting angry.

Tim Smith

9. We have three children, ages fifteen, thirteen and eleven, who constantly fight and argue with one another, and it's driving us crazy. We've tried talking to them about getting along with each other, we've had family meetings, we've tried punishing them, but nothing seems to work. They insist that they don't like each other, which is just heartbreaking to us. Is this normal?

Yes, it's normal, although not inevitable. Some siblings actually seem to get along fine with each other. Whether they do or not usually has a lot to do with the ages of the children, their genders, personalities, living conditions and many other factors. But the reality of sibling relationships is that turmoil is normal. That's because children of the same family are not there by choice. Unlike spouses and friends, siblings do not choose one another. They are brought together by providence, and sometimes they find this totally unfair and unacceptable. They demonstrate this by how they treat each other. The good news is that most siblings eventually put their childhood differences aside as adults and, more often than not, become friends, or at least learn how to be civil toward each other.

You can't really eliminate sibling rivalries or force children to like each other, but you can put a few rules in place to help govern the conflict. For example:

- No hitting, kicking, gouging or poking each other in the eyes.
- No throwing or swinging objects of any kind.

■ No using foul language or calling each other derogatory names.

By being clear on these rules, you can then be clear about the consequences of breaking them. Which brings up one additional rule:

■ If any of these rules are broken, all three of you will be punished equally regardless of who was at fault.

That will save you the indignity of having to listen to each of them blaming each other, tattling on each other, arguing over who was at fault and so on.

Because siblings love to watch each other suffer, they will often see it as their solemn duty to immediately report every rule infraction by the other to the nearest authority: "Mom, Nick poured his milk down the sink!" "Dad, Joshua left the light on in the garage." To reduce the frequency of such reports, some parents have instituted a tattling rule that provides either (1) a reward for the person being tattled on (even if what they did was wrong), or (2) a punishment for everyone, including the tattler. Use at your own discretion.

Sibling squabbles are to be expected, and most of the time the best thing to do is nothing at all. Of course, if someone is in real danger of getting hurt, you may need to step into the fray, but otherwise don't interfere unless you have to. Just say, "I don't want to hear about it" and walk away. Don't be so quick to assume the role of referee or judge in your kids' disputes. Every time you intervene, you teach them to rely on you to solve all their problems for them. What they need to learn is how to solve their own problems and to get along with people they don't like.

Wayne Rice

2

EMOTIONS

10. *We are having trouble responding to our teenager's moodiness. He will suddenly get very angry or very depressed for no apparent reason. The next day he may be fine and quite pleasant to be around. But then he'll turn sullen or mean-spirited, not like himself at all. We've tried to talk with him to find out the cause of his mood swings, but he doesn't give us much information. Should we seek professional help?*

First the good news: moodiness is a normal characteristic of adolescence, particularly for young teens who have so many new hormones flying through their bodies at breakneck speed. They are experiencing new emotions at an intensity level they are not used to, and they usually have no idea why.

Boys in particular (not to mention most men!) tend to have quite a limited emotional vocabulary. So when you ask, "Why are you acting so moody?" your son probably doesn't yet have language to explain what he is going through. Probing questions about his moodiness are likely to add feelings of shame (or stupidity) to his already negative emotions. In other words, your trying to understand him by asking a series of why questions can actually increase his moodiness.

In short, he's moody because he's a teenager. The best place to focus your efforts is in the area of your response to his moodiness. If, for example, he has a responsibility for doing the dishes, but he refuses with an attitude of disrespect because he "just doesn't feel like it," it is important for you to respond to his behavior, not his mood. Give him a choice between doing dishes or staying home for the weekend, or a choice between speaking respectfully or not having access to the computer for the next day.

You can wear yourself out trying to figure out your son's moods, but you'll only wind up feeling more powerless. As you have likely already realized, talking and asking your son lots of questions about his moodiness makes little or no progress. Instead, act more and talk less when it comes to responding to your son's moodiness. At some point, you may discover that it would be helpful for him to see a counselor, but don't start there. Start with the place you've got the most leverage: your own actions.

Mark DeVries

11. *I'm worried about our teenager's self-image. She's a little bit over-weight and doesn't seem to have a lot of friends. Her grades are also slipping. We try not to push her too hard or to make comments about her appearance, mainly because we don't want to make things worse. I've heard that teens with low self-esteem are more vulnerable to peer pressure and self-destructive behavior, and I'm concerned about our daughter. Any suggestions?*

It's good that you are concerned about your daughter's self-image, and yes, there are some actions you can take that may be helpful.

You are right about accepting her and avoiding comments about her weight, her grades or her choice of friends. She needs to know that she is loved and accepted unconditionally by her parents. If she asks for help with her weight or grades, then provide it. But it's important that before you give a suggestion, you first ask her what she feels she should do. Your job is not to solve her difficulties but to assist and support her in solving them.

We can't give our teenagers self-worth. That must be earned and gained as they learn to become self-sufficient. Our job is to treat them as if they are capable and give them opportunities for success. This comes in part from a positive family attitude built on acceptance and affirmation.

Affirm your daughter whenever possible. As we like to say at our Understanding Your Teenager seminars, "Catch her in the act of doing something good." Affirmation is not flattery but encourages good behavior. It's specific and to the point. For example, it's better to say, "You showed great leadership today by helping the youth group organize next summer's mission trip," than to say, "You're the smartest kid in the whole youth group!"

Work with her to take on some responsibilities and to be helpful at home, church and even in the community. Teenagers who are giving of themselves think a whole lot less about their self-image than those who are not involved. Further, when we imply to our teen that they can handle a responsibility, they handle it. When we imply to them that they can't handle it, they don't. As they gain the courage to try new things, and even sometimes make mistakes, we can create an environment for healthy growth and help them avoid developing destructive patterns.

As you accept her she will know she's loved by the special people in her life. As you affirm her she will recognize she has many positive life skills. She will begin to take control of her life, take on responsibilities and make decisions that will affect her life. It's in these qualities that she will gain her self-worth.

Jim Green

12. *Our fifteen-year-old son has a bad attitude about everything. No matter what we say or do, he disagrees or makes negative comments. It's starting to wear us down. What can we do to make him change his attitude?*

A teenager's bad attitude can get old real quick. You'd love to have your son change 180 degrees and suddenly be filled with joy and positive comments. Some teens, however, seem to think that it's their job to be negative. So some of the time you'll just have to grit your teeth and say nothing. Try not to overreact to the little comments and criticisms. Most of them are harmless. Concern yourself more with his behavior than his attitude. It's always better to get good behavior with a bad attitude than bad behavior with a good attitude.

Perhaps you and your son could go out for a meal and just talk (teens usually have a pretty positive attitude about food). Without being overly critical, try to explain how you feel, how his bad attitude sometimes makes him look bad (to family and others) and how we can choose to have a positive attitude, even when things aren't going so great. Life throws a lot at us that we can't change—the weather, family, world events, referees'/umpires' decisions, traffic jams—but we can choose how we react to those unchangeable events. You should also explain that you don't expect him to always be "up," or to always be in a good mood. Everyone has ups and downs, good days and bad days. But we should strive to have more positive days than bad ones. People like positive people . . . so try to be one!

Don't just do all the talking, however. Be sure to listen to him and allow him to vent if he needs to do that, or to reveal whatever issues might be causing his bad attitude. He may just have a need to express to you how he is feeling. If you listen to him, he'll listen more to you.

Dave Veerman

13. *We aren't sure if our seventeen-year-old's behavior is normal or not. Lately he has totally lost interest in school. He's a senior and I've heard about "senioritis," but this is bad. I'm afraid he's going to flunk a couple of classes that he needs in order to graduate. We don't think he's doing drugs or anything like that. Is this normal?*

It's not unusual for seniors to lose interest in school, particularly during the second semester. They often reason, *What difference does school make now? Colleges won't be looking at my grades. I've worked hard . . . now it's time to relax.*

Honestly, in some cases, they are right. They may have already been accepted into college, and they may not even need the credits from the current term to graduate. But most seniors still need the credits, and *all* seniors need to keep up their self-discipline and study skills. Things become even more challenging in college!

In your son's case, I can think of three things that might be going on. First, he might be overwhelmed with the subjects or workload of his classes. Some senior-level courses take a quantum leap in complexity and amount of work. He may not be able to handle this jump. You may need to get him a tutor or talk to his teacher about the situation and get his or her perspective. In many cases, teens fail because they simply don't turn in their work. A lot of times, they do it; they just don't get it turned in! Help organize his day into two-hour study periods where he does nothing but homework. Even if he argues he doesn't have homework, have him outline the

GO AHEAD, PUSH!

Accepting our teenagers is important, but it's also important to give them standards. It is too easy to accept below-ability performance in an attempt to be affirming.

More than once I reminded our sons that their high school classes were not Harvard Law School and so they ought to be able to perform a little better. This encouraged them to work closer to their potential.

Kendra Smiley

text, read ahead or organize his notebook for the full two hours. Do allow short breaks for food so he can keep his blood sugar up.

Second, he may need accommodations for the classes he is having difficulty with. Again, talk to the teacher about this. He may need to sit in the front, have his assignments written and explained after class, or other, more extensive adjustments. If he is having the same problem in all or most of his classes, you might consider having him tested for a learning disability. I know of dozens of teens who did not know they had a disability until their senior year when they couldn't keep up.

Third, he may be afraid of leaving high school and the protection and innocence that it offers. He may sense that "all of my friends are going away," and experience loss at a variety of levels. If this is true, he may need to process these feelings with a trusted friend, youth worker or counselor. You might be too close to the situation for him to talk with you.

Of course, he simply may be lazy. If that's the case, say, "Your job right now is to be a student and bring home passing grades. If you can't do that, I will have to prepare you for a different path in life— one that doesn't require brains, but brawn. So I'll help you by giving you more chores around here to make your back strong since that seems to be the career path you are on." I have suggested this several times, and it's amazing how the boys get those grades up when they face the prospect of manual labor!

Tim Smith

14. *One thing we do not allow in our home is disrespect. My wife and I get very angry when our fifteen-year-old talks back and says things that are disrespectful to us. How should I respond when my teenager acts this way?*

Sooner or later you'll probably hear your angry teenager yell something like "You're stupid!" or "I hate you!" or "Nobody else has a jerk
like you for a parent!" Or worse. They often lack the maturity to think

DEFINING DISRESPECT

While disrespectful behavior is common with teenagers, it should not be "normalized." Parents who react to the disrespectful teenager in anger or defense are being equally disrespectful to the teen, and neither behavior is necessary or acceptable.

It is possible that your teenager is not aware that his or her behavior has been disrespectful. Given that possibility, the first thing you must do is explain what you consider appropriate and inappropriate, or disrespectful, behavior. Your teenager needs to know the parameters, what is acceptable and what is unacceptable. It might be helpful to make a list of those things you consider to be disrespectful and post it for your teenager to read. For example:

The following behaviors are considered "disrespectful" and are subject to severe consequences:

- *Saying no or refusing to do what you are asked to do, like picking up your things, washing the dishes, feeding the cat, etc.*
- *Using swear words or "put downs" of any kind.*
- *Mimicking (making fun of) either of your parents in an unflattering way.*
- *Telling a lie to either of your parents.*
- *Throwing things, slamming doors or any other kind of physical outburst.*

In addition to explaining what constitutes disrespectful behavior, the punishment for choosing that behavior should also be determined and announced. It should not be administered retroactively, however. Don't punish your teenagers for the offense that occurred before the discussion. Give them the benefit of the doubt. Assume they did not realize that their behavior was disrespectful.

How do you establish the consequence for disrespect? In part it is determined by the attitude of your son or daughter. If the negative behavior was done in obvious defiance, the punishment should be more severe than if it was merely a careless mistake. This should also be discussed in advance.

Remember that the rules for respect should be mutual. They are in place for everyone in the home. Your behavior should be a model of respect for your children to follow.

Kendra Smiley

before they speak. But if you scream back, "You ungrateful little brat! You're grounded for a month!" you may be acting less mature than your teen.

Teens will challenge us and make statements that sting, but they are not helped when we react and respond in anger and defensiveness. Remember that these outbursts of disrespect are signs of immaturity, hormones and impulsiveness. They are totally normal for teens. If teenagers didn't react with these obnoxious eruptions, they wouldn't be teenagers. But when they lose control, it is absolutely necessary that we don't.

How do we maintain control in the heat of battle? Remember not to take your teen or their tantrums too seriously or too personally. If you were in their shoes, you might be tempted to act the same way. So step back from the emotion (the one that makes you want to strangle them) and coolly say, "So what?" (pause) "You still need to do what I've asked you to do." Part of parenting teens effectively is acting. You will need to act like it doesn't bother you when it actually does. Focus on their behavior and the request you have made, not on the accusations and name calling that are thrown at you.

When parents tell me that they want their teen to "respect them," I tell them to give it up. When we focus on the vague emotion of respect, we rarely make any progress. If we deal with obedience and behavior, however, we can get somewhere. When you start preaching the respect-and-bad-attitude sermon, the relationship with your teen is bound to become worse! So focus on obedience and don't worry about attitude and respect for a while. In time, you will get compliance, along with a better attitude and respect for being such a mature parent in control.

Tim Smith

15. *Should we worry when our daughter threatens suicide? I really don't think she's serious, but she has brought it up several times in the last few months when we've had disagreements.*

Threats of suicide should always be taken seriously. Suicide is one of the leading causes of death among teenagers. While you may not believe that she is serious, you should always take her seriously.

How can you tell if your daughter is seriously considering suicide? There are a number of warning signs that professionals use to determine suicidal behavior (see sidebar on p. 46). If these are apparent in your daughter, seek help for her immediately.

If the only time your daughter mentions suicide is during or following a disagreement, she is probably trying to send you a message. She may be crying out for affection, attention or help. She may be fighting for her independence or expressing frustration with the limits that you have set for her. Sometimes teenagers will threaten suicide in an argument because they believe parents will give up or give in. Such a threat is used as a weapon in the heat of battle. Don't panic, but observe her and monitor any degree of isolation or other warning signs. Again, threats of suicide should never be taken lightly.

Your response to her is important. If she is threatening suicide as her only way of handling conflict, you may need to spend more time with her and work on the relationship you have with her. Learn to listen to her more and find out what is causing her frustration, anger or feelings of depression. There may be some changes that you need to make regarding the issues that you fight over with your daughter. You may need to get some help realigning communication between you and your daughter.

When you daughter threatens suicide, make sure she knows that you are listening. Ask her some questions: "Are you really considering suicide?" If she answers yes, ask if she has a plan for carrying it out. How does she intend to do it? Suicide is a process that includes a great deal of painstaking thought on the teenager's part. It is seldom random. If she truly has a plan for committing suicide, she will more than likely let you know in order to prove that she is serious. If she does, get her help immediately.

If she doesn't have a suicide plan but seems depressed, get her a thorough medical intake, including blood work and stress tests, to determine if there is any chemical imbalance that could be triggering emotional swings. Many teens (and adults) have feelings of "I wish I were dead." If your family doctor diagnoses clinical depression or some kind of chemical imbalance, he or she will probably refer you to a psychologist or psychiatrist for further tests and perhaps medication. Antidepressants can help, but they always need to be used in conjunction with counseling.

The bottom line is this: the mention of suicide should always be taken seriously. Pray, love, care, and if need be, seek

SUICIDE WARNING SIGNS

Your teenager may be contemplating suicide when these warning signs appear:

- outbursts of anger
- problems at home, school, church
- withdrawal from family and long hours alone
- sudden change in behavior, especially school-related changes (grades) and changes in relationships
- symptoms of depression, sadness
- drug and alcohol use
- change of sleeping and eating habits
- running away
- unwanted pregnancy
- loss (broken friendship, dating relationship)
- giving away of possessions
- obsession with songs and poems dealing with death and suicide
- talking about death and suicide
- ongoing periods of aloneness and isolation

Many teens experience these warning signs without being suicidal. For example, not every depressed teen is suicidal. Not every teen who is cut from the basketball team is suicidal. Ongoing signs of depression, however, should be carefully evaluated, and professional and medical help may be your next step.

David Olshine

help for you and your daughter to learn better coping and communication skills.

David Olshine

16. My son is sixteen, and he always seems to be angry. Is it normal for my teenager to express so much anger? Could there be something wrong?

Anger is complex. There can be many reasons for an angry outburst from a teenager. Rather than responding with anger ourselves, our job is to listen and respond in a way that defuses the anger. What is behind your son's anger?

- Is he suffering from low self-esteem?

- Is he having problems at school?

- Has there been a problem in the family?

- Does he feel cared for and loved?

- Is he hurting about a relationship or a rejection?

- Could he be feeling lonely?

- Is he embarrassed or feeling guilty about something?

Where there is anger, there is usually pain. Your goal should be to identify the pain and help your teenager deal with it in a positive way.

Angry teens often hurl the accusation, "You just don't understand me." This is a key issue. Do they know we've heard what they said? Do they know we are trying to understand? By listening (without reacting) to a teen communicate his or her feelings, a parent can positively penetrate a teen's anger so that both of you can move toward greater understanding.

Listen closely to what your son says when he expresses his anger. He could be trying to tell you something about the cause of his anger.

When we take seriously what an angry teen is saying, we send this message: "You are an important person and I value you."

Allow your teen to voice his or her thoughts completely. Be careful about jumping to a conclusion, giving your advice or opinion, or trying to solve his problems for him. Ask, "What do you think you should do?" or, "What are your options?" Most teens just lack the skills to work through their problems. Self-discovery is the best kind of learning.

Avoid arguing with your angry teenager. Sixteen-year-olds rarely understand things from a parent's point of view. If he threatens to run away from home if you don't let him do something, don't waste your time trying to talk him out of it. Instead, you might say, "Well, that's an option." Then let him consider the consequences of his possible decision.

Defusing a potentially explosive situation is not letting them roll over you. You have rights too. They must share with you in a controlled manner and with respect. (Sometimes it's best to wait to talk

ANGER IN POP CULTURE

Many teenagers express a great deal of anger as their way of identifying with today's popular culture. If you haven't noticed, most pictures you see today of teenagers, rock stars, teen idols and so on are not the smiling faces of Happy Days youth. It's "in" to snarl at the camera and look as angry and rebellious as possible.

There's no question that much of the music that kids are listening to these days is filled with anger, hate and hopelessness. While this is nothing new, today's hip-hop culture tends to feed on unusually negative images of violence and death. Much of the self-mutilation, drug abuse and other risk-taking behaviors we see in today's young people stems from a worldview that promotes anger and rebellion as "cool."

Some teenagers, however, become obsessed with blatantly angry and rebellious music as a way of identifying their own pain, hurt and depression. Observant parents and other adults should pay close attention to these kids and help them deal with their feelings in a positive way.

Wayne Rice

with your teen after their intense emotions have passed.) The great irony of anger is that the more forceful its expression, the less effective its message is for you and them.

The most important part of anger is listening, not discipline. When we respond with something like "Go to your room!" the anger is not resolved. This discipline might seem to control the situation temporarily, but the teenager is in his room just getting angrier. Making him go to his room leads to increased feelings of loneliness. Taking privileges away leads to more anger. Withholding tenderness and affection causes him to turn to others. Forcing him to sit through lectures and sermons pretty much guarantees that he won't listen.

Again, being punished rarely takes away the anger.

This might be a good time to take an inventory of your relationship with your teen. Maybe both of you have drifted apart. Spend some quality time with him, take an interest in the things that are important to him, and tell him he is loved.

Jim Green

3

COMMUNICATION

17. *Do parents have a right to search their teenager's room? I believe I do—but my fourteen-year-old daughter insists that her room is off limits to me and that she has a right to her privacy. In her view, I can't even enter her room without permission, let alone conduct a search. Who's right on this issue?*

First of all, assuming you are the owner of your house (which most likely includes your daughter's bedroom), you absolutely do have the right to every square inch of it. It belongs to you, not her.

However, your daughter is correct when she says that she has a right to her privacy. That's a basic human right that should be respected by everyone, including parents. But she also needs to understand that rights come with responsibilities. If she thinks she can do whatever she wants in her bedroom, she is mistaken.

For example, every person in the United States has a right to privacy in their own homes unless their home is being used for selling drugs, building bombs or conducting other illegal activities. Some neighborhoods have restrictions that prevent private homes from being used as a commercial business. Others prohibit certain kinds of noise or have standards regarding yard maintenance, garbage collection and so on. In exchange for the right to privacy, we usually have to accept certain responsibilities that go with it. Likewise, there are house rules that don't stop at your daughter's bedroom door. She is required to abide by them. If she does, there will be no reason to search her room.

As a rule of thumb, parents should respect their teenager's privacy and resist the urge to go snooping through their stuff. A search motivated by mere curiosity will do nothing but undermine trust and communication. If your daughter has given you no real reason to be suspicious, then it's best to give her and her possessions the same respect that you would expect from her. The more respect you give your children, the more respectfully they will behave.

On the other hand, if your daughter has been lying to you consistently, breaking curfew, skipping school, or otherwise engaging in behavior that is harmful to herself or others, then you have not only the right to search her room but the responsibility to do so. That's something even a teenager can understand. What if you search and find nothing? Then your daughter probably deserves a confession and an apology. Trust, after all, works both ways.

Wayne Rice

---

18. *Our son is by nature a quiet person, and now that he's a teenager, it seems he doesn't want to talk at all. How can I get him to talk to me?*

The most important thing to remember is not to force (or try to force) your teenage son to talk. Instead, create situations where talking to one another is natural. One scenario is to work together. The key word there is *together.* Don't assign work to him and then supervise it. Work with your son. Another way is to play together. What does your son like to do? Our youngest loved to play baseball, and my husband and he played hours of "pitch and catch." Does your son like animals or video games or shooting baskets? Play with him, and conversations will naturally occur. Don't make talk the primary goal. Play with your son and any conversation that occurs is a bonus.

It is also helpful to remember to engage your son in talking about topics that are interesting to him. Keep in mind that communication is a two-way process. Too often parents lecture their teenagers instead of talking with them.

Kendra Smiley

19. When I try to talk to my teenager, we always get into an argument and end up shouting at each other. This is very frustrating for me. How can I have a conversation with my teenager without things turning ugly?

Take a few minutes and analyze these arguments. Where do they occur? You may find that home is the prime location, or maybe it's in the car. Try talking with your teenager somewhere else. Something as simple as changing the environment can often change the atmosphere.

You may find other consistent factors: time of day, certain people in the room, specific topics and so forth. If that's the case, use those as warning signals and try to avoid discussions at those times or, at least, tread carefully.

Whatever the case, in every conversation, try hard to keep your cool and not overreact. It's easy to get sidetracked by a snide comment, disrespectful posture or bad attitude. Ignore those and stick to the facts, explaining as calmly as you can your thoughts and feelings. And when your teenager responds, listen carefully and feed back what was just expressed. You could say, for example, "You sound very frustrated. What I hear you saying is that you don't enjoy our trips to your grandparents' house any more and would rather not go. Is that right?" Clarification can only help. It probably won't end the disagreement, but at least you'll both be talking about the same thing.

Having said all this, I need to add that arguments are inevitable with teenagers. Somehow they get the idea that it's their job to disagree with mom and dad. Actually, they're pushing for independence, for making their own decisions, and they're learning how to think. For a few years, they don't want to be you. So relax a bit and enjoy the show. I'm not saying that you have to give up and give in—just don't make a big deal out of everything.

Dave Veerman

20. *Whenever I try to talk to my son, he thinks I'm yelling at him. BUT I'M NOT YELLING! (Just kidding.) Seriously, I don't raise my voice. I'm just trying to make sure he understands what I'm saying. Still, he thinks I'm yelling at him. What's wrong with this picture?*

Your son is good. Sounds like he has become a master in the fine art of deflecting criticism. And it sounds like it's working.

He may have discovered that there are times when his only defense is a good offense. When he feels criticism coming on, he has learned how to stop you in your tracks with his own preemptive strikes.

Other kids may use different words, like "You never listen to me!" "I'm always the one who gets picked on, aren't I?" and the ever popular, "You don't trust me, do you?" But regardless of the words, the objective from the teenager's point of view is the same: neutralize negative feedback by paralyzing the parent with criticism first.

But don't trade in your parenting badge quite yet. When you have a message to deliver to your son, pick your battles wisely and deliver the message, even if imperfectly.

At the same time, it is quite possible that when you express concerns to your son you are doing it with an intensity you are not even aware of. And, in fact, he really may feel like you are yelling at him (which really does get in the way of hearing the message you're trying to deliver). The greatest leverage you have in influencing your son's behavior is in changing your own. A child learns a willingness to grow in response to coaching from parents when that child grows up in an environment in which such growth is modeled by the adults in his or her life. So when your son tells you that you are yelling, you've got a window of opportunity to model the kind of response to criticism you'd like to see in him.

My wife has learned to call my intensity the "blow fish." My eyebrows raise, my voice tightens, and she can smell the anger in my tone. Sometimes I have to trust her instincts when she tells me I am becoming the "blow fish," even when I can't see it myself. When it comes to the way we deliver our messages to our children, the Bible specifically speaks to fathers when it says, "Fathers, do not embitter your children, or they will become discouraged" (Colossians 3:21). Although you don't want to be manipulated by your son's Captain Deflector costume, you may also need to get a reality check on your own communication style.

You might try this response with your son: "Wow, I was totally unaware that I was yelling. Let me try again. Is this better?" And then simply respond to your son's feedback in the way you would like for him to respond to yours. You don't have to be sidetracked from actually delivering the message you came to deliver. But it is essential that you not blow up the bridge of your relationship with your son just to get your point across.

And make sure, too, that you finish any critical comments by asking specifically for the behavior you are looking for. Parents who say, "Your attitude stinks, and you need to do something about it," can leave their sons or daughters confused about what they actually need to do. Much better to end the conversation with, "So I'd like to ask that when you are at the dinner table you not roll your eyes or sigh, and that you stay at the table until we have all eaten (or at least until *Survivor* comes on)."

Mark DeVries

21. Okay, I've read your book on understanding teenagers. Now, how can I help my two teenagers to understand ME?

If you want your kids to know and understand *you,* just spend more time with them. They will learn a lot. Someone said, "With teenagers, more is going to be caught than taught." Modeling is the key. By observation, your teenagers will learn more about you and about your values than any other way. For example, if I want to teach my daughter that I trust God with my life, I need to allow her to watch how I respond to tough situations. If I want my son to understand that forgiveness is an important biblical value, I want him to experience me saying, "Son, I was wrong for screaming at you. It is my problem. Will you forgive me?"

Second, share your life with your kids by talking about your life. Let them hear your story. Use teachable moments, like mealtimes, to talk about your life. The Israelites were always talking about their deliverance from Egypt as a way to help their children understand their heritage. One of the key words for a Jewish person in the Scriptures is *remember.* Storytelling is a way of remembering. If you want your kids to understand who you are, tell your stories, both past and present. Communicate your struggles (with wisdom and discernment), your joys, your fears, your passions. You don't have to tell your kids everything, of course. Age-appropriateness is always in order.

Here's another suggestion: Get your teenager a copy of Wayne Rice's book *Read This Book or You're Grounded* or Ken Davis's book

How to Live with Your Parents (Without Losing Your Mind) (both published by Zondervan). These books are written in a teen-friendly style, and they are both designed to help teenagers better understand parents and the issues they face.

Don't expect your kid to run up to you before bedtime and say, "I really understand you now." Even though they are learning a lot about you and what's important to you, they don't want you to know they are!

David Olshine

22. *I have a good relationship with our son right now, but as he gets older, I fear that might change. How can I keep a good relationship with him throughout his teen years?*

There is no need to fear if you truly have a good relationship now. Teenagers do not automatically rebel. They definitely mature and seek autonomy, but rebellion is not necessary or inevitable. If your interactions are pleasant right now in his preteen years, there is no reason to believe that your son won't want that interaction to continue.

One thing that will help your son and you maintain that good relationship is to be predictable in your interaction with him. If you are not "the comedienne" at home, do not try to assume that role around his friends. Your teenager does not want to be surprised when you are around him. Be yourself. That's the way he likes you.

Kendra Smiley

23. *Lately I've noticed that my teenager avoids me at every turn. When I walk into the living room, for example, he gets up and leaves. When I ask if he'd like to do something with me, he's busy or just doesn't want to do it. It's like I have some contagious disease. I'm beginning to think that my teenager hates me. Am I being paranoid or is this normal?*

Yes, this attitude of separation is normal in teen development. They desire independence and want to be their own person. And yes, you're probably somewhat paranoid. You could be reading into his actions things that are not there.

Now back to the normal side of separation. Teenagers are growing into adults. They feel they need to make the decisions for their life. They desire their own space. They want control. So here is the conflict. You still are a parent, and need to be! Yet teenagers want the right to live their own life.

Don't avoid your teenager, even when he avoids you. Open up the doors to good communication and be proactive about your relationship right away. Find time when you can be with your son to talk and allow him to share what he is thinking and feeling. Be careful not to react or to rush to explain your feelings . . . just listen.

He still needs parental guidance in many areas and may sometimes desperately crave a hug or a show of love from you. Ironically, he may see this as a weakness on his part and unconsciously try to force separation by lashing out at you.

However, it's possible that something is going on in his life that might be more than just the normal need for adolescent separation. You might ask yourself some of these questions: *Am I fun to live with? Do I jump all over him as soon as he walks through the door? Am I smothering him, wanting his constant presence? Am I asking too many questions and talking too much?* Or could he be afraid you're going to find out about something that's going on in his life? It's obvious by your question that something is causing him to push you away and separate himself.

I am a strong believer that when situations become unhealthy or troublesome, it's wise to involve a counselor of some type. Someone your son might know and respect would be helpful. It could be a close family friend, a coach or his youth pastor. If the behavior continues I'd suggest a professional counselor who works with teens and families. They can be very helpful.

You are right to be concerned. Even though your son seems resistant to a close relationship with you right now, do whatever it takes to restore and build a relationship of mutual respect, communication and love.

Jim Green

24. *I've been trying to encourage my teenager by letting him do more things on his own and to succeed or fail on his own. But I still think he needs direction and guidance from me. How can I do this without making him feel incompetent?*

At our Understanding Your Teenager seminars, we like to tell parents, "When your children become teenagers, they will fire you as their parent but hire you back as a consultant." It sounds like it's time for you to get hired.

I can think of three experiences that can motivate your teenager to hire you as his consultant: frustration, boredom and lack of success. You see, without a little discomfort, teenagers will almost always be satisfied with the way things are. They will assume that they already know the secrets of making life work. They will look to their inexperienced friends for counsel, believing that advice from parents is the last thing they need.

Parents make a big mistake when they treat their children's boredom, frustration and lack of success as enemies rather than allies. In fact, the whole notion of kids learning through consequences is based on the power of these three allies. For example, a "no TV, phone or computer" consequence can leverage a teenager's boredom in such a way that motivates change.

If you find that your advice-giving conversations are met with rolling eyes and exasperated sighs, chances are you're giving too much unsolicited advice. Apart from safety issues and moral issues, your son's failures can actually work in his favor. His feeling incompetent may actually be the first step in his developing an appetite for competence.

But until he asks, the best direction you can give your son is clear and firm expectations about behavior, with clear consequences when he doesn't follow through on a commitment or speaks in ways that are disrespectful. Offering consequences (with a smile) in these situations is the best way to protect your relationship from the corrosive effect of the advice-giving/resistance cycle.

Mark DeVries

THE FOUR PHASES OF EASE

Some time ago I learned a simple four-step process for transferring skills or responsibilities to others called "The Four Phases of Ease." By using this process, or one like it, you can teach anyone (including your kids) how to do what you do. It is based on the idea that you don't want to dump too much responsibility on them too soon, nor do you want to discourage them by not giving them enough responsibility when they are ready for it. Briefly, here are the four steps:

- *Phase One: "I do it, you watch."*
- *Phase Two: "We do it together."*
- *Phase Three: "You do it, I watch."*
- *Phase Four: "You do it, I go do something else."*

As you can see, each step gives more and more responsibility to the student, while the teacher does less and less. Our goal should be to work ourselves out of a job as parents, and this process can help us reach that goal.

Wayne Rice

25. *I can't help myself. Our teenager drives me batty and I lose my temper. Do you have any suggestions?*

It's certainly understandable. Teenagers know which buttons to push to get certain reactions from us. They can be very aggravating at times. But it's best not to play the game. Here are some dos and don'ts:

- DO stay calm.
- DO say how you feel.
- DO try to identify the cause for your feelings and reactions.
- DON'T call names, swear or belittle your teenager.
- DON'T react to a reaction, no matter how outrageous or loud.
- DON'T go off on a tangent—stay the course.

If you do lose your temper and get into a shouting match or say things you shouldn't say, be sure to apologize later. No one's perfect, as all parents of teenagers know from experience.

Dave Veerman

26. *Is it just me, or do teenagers have more trouble getting along with their moms than their dads? My husband seems oblivious to it all. Help!*

Not all teenagers have trouble getting along with their moms, but many of them do—for at least two reasons. The first is that moms are often the ones who are there when teenagers are letting off steam. Moms who spend more time with their kids than their husbands simply make an easy target. Don't take this too personally; it's normal.

But there's another reason that may require some change on your part. It has been my experience that moms tend to baby their children and treat them as though they are not as mature as they actually are. Dads, on the other hand, are more likely to allow their teenagers to have increased freedom and responsibility. If that is the case, your teenager will be more likely to gravitate to a relationship with your husband. It is important to work together as husband and wife to give feedback to one another. Your husband can help you evaluate your interaction with your teenager and alert you if you are not promoting maturity. Allow and encourage your teenager to accept responsibility.

Kendra Smiley

27. *I know it's normal for teenagers to make mistakes, and I know that parents need to be forgiving. But how can I show forgiveness to my teen when he just repeats the same mistake over and over?*

It's frustrating, isn't it? We hand down our commandments and then our children—who we've created—live as if we've never uttered a word! Doesn't the Bible say, "Honor your father and mother"? Don't they get it? What part of "Thou shalt not (fill in the blank: stay out past midnight, have your friends over when no parents are home, leave your towel on the floor)" do they not understand? It's not just frustrating; it's downright sinful!

And, of course, it's only when we begin to understand the outrage of that kind of sinful behavior that we can begin to understand the amazing grace that God extends to every single one of us.

Not to overspiritualize, but your question sounds a lot like one Jesus was asked by Peter: " 'Lord, how many times shall I forgive my brother when he sins against me? Up to seven times?' Jesus answered, 'I tell you, not seven times, but seventy-seven times' " (Matthew 18:21-22).

Maybe it's because we had two children and everything was just naturally split in half, but my daughters were constantly arguing about fairness. No matter how many times we discussed "getting along with each other" and "being kind to your sister," there were aggravating protests about justice and fairness.

"That's not fair!"

"Ohmygosh, that is, like, so unfair!"

One day, fed up with life in The People's Court, I turned to my daughters in exasperation and said through squinty eyes and gritted teeth, "You know what, ladies? You'd better think twice right now before you demand justice. Because I'm telling you, neither one of you wants what you really deserve."

I mention this because at the core of forgiveness is the clear realization that we have ourselves been forgiven—not just once, not just seven times, but many, many times over! My children don't really want justice and fairness, and if I'm honest, neither do I. What I really want, what I really need, is grace. And in response to the grace I receive from my Father in heaven, I am commanded to extend grace to others—even those sometimes exasperating teenagers that live with us. In his prayer to the Father, Jesus put it this way: "Forgive us our sins, / for we also forgive everyone who sins against us" (Luke 11:4; see also Matthew 6:12-15). I suppose it could be paraphrased a bit to read, "Forgive us our sins, as we forgive our sons."

Let me add, though, that to forgive is not to ignore. Forgiveness is canceling a debt; it is not acting as if the debt does not exist. God did not ignore the debt of our sin; he sent his Son, Jesus, to pay it by his death. That means as a parent you must couple your forgiveness with consistent discipline. Disobedience comes with a price tag.

If your teenager comes home an hour past curfew, you don't pout, you don't greet him with icy silence, you don't threaten to sell his tuba. You might simply say, "Okay, you brought the car home late. That doesn't mean I give up on you or that I don't love you or even that I don't like you." (In other words, "What you have done is not unforgivable.") "But it does mean that you won't be able to use the car next weekend." (In other words, "What you have done is a violation of our house rules and you must answer for that.") That's a statement that communicates forgiveness. But it does it in a way that communicates to your son, "I forgive you, but just because grace is freely given, that doesn't mean it's cheap."

Duffy Robbins

28. *I've blown it as a parent. For years I set a very bad example for my children and was abusive to them in many ways. I don't blame my kids for not wanting to have a relationship with me, but I do love them, and more than anything in the world I want to start being the kind of father they deserve. Are there some steps that I can take to become a good parent after so many years of being a bad one?*

The only way to restore a relationship with your kids is to take it one day and one child and one step at a time. There's no sure-fire formula or magic pill. It will take work and patience and a ton of prayer.

Have a heart-to-heart talk with each child, one-on-one. The best place for this is out of the house. You could go for breakfast, take a walk in the park, go fishing or go shopping; do something that the child would enjoy. During this time apologize, say what you'd like to be as a father, and ask for help in becoming that kind of person. Say that you want to be the kind of father that God wants: tough at times but tender, responsible, strong, hard working, kind, caring. Reassure the child of your love and that you want to follow the pattern of love outlined in 1 Corinthians 13:4-7 (read the passage together). Ask for suggestions on what you can do to improve. You don't have to agree to all of them, but listen respectfully without reacting, and take notes.

Your quest to become a better parent needs to start there, with your kids. But you should enlist others in the project. Find a Christian father or couple who you respect, and ask if he (they) would mentor you, holding you accountable and moving you in the right direction.

Dave Veerman

29. *Yesterday my son and I got into an argument that turned ugly very quickly. He used some bad language and said he hated me and wished I was dead. As you can imagine, I've been very hurt by this and am at a loss as to how I should respond. We haven't spoken since this happened. I am a single mother. What should I do?*

Teenagers often use words as weapons. The meaning of the words they say is less important than the impact they have. For that reason, it's best not to take what they say too literally or too personally. Remember that an outburst like this probably has more to do with your son than you.

Conflict is normal with teenagers, particularly over issues of power and control. Arguments only make things worse. You should never argue with a teenager, because there's no way you can win. Save your breath and just do what you know is best for your son and your family.

As a single mom you have a difficult job. It's not easy for single moms to raise sons by themselves. It's possible that your son is expressing anger toward you because he is resentful about not having a dad around. He may be lashing out without really understanding why. Perhaps you can find a way to help him connect with an older male in his life who is willing to become a role model and mentor to him.

When your teenager gets emotional and uses words to hurt you, be careful that you are not lured into the same kind of disrespectful behavior. Try to stay calm and say something like, "I understand what you are saying, and if I were in your shoes, I'd probably feel the same way. But I'm in my shoes, and my decision still stands. I'm sorry." Remember that respect is a two-way street, and your son needs to be taught how to be respectful. Your behavior is the best teacher.

When parents get angry, it can also incite feelings of insecurity in young minds. They perceive that our anger and frustration is caused by our inability to control the situation. There is nothing more powerful in an argument than when parents are in control of their emotions, objective, rational and dignified.

Take the initiative to sit with your son and open the door to talking. Tell him you are sorry for losing control and saying the things you said. Hopefully he will apologize too. The longer it takes to begin communicating, the more anger will build up on both sides. The Bible says, "Do not let the sun go down while you are still angry" (Ephesians 4:26). When you talk things out, there is a lot less need to act things out.

Jim Green

DATING AND SEXUALITY

30. *At what age should I begin talking to my children about sex? I don't want to put ideas in their heads.*

You should begin very early to talk with your children about sex, as long as your comments are age-appropriate. Certainly you should begin by about third or fourth grade, but children will probably ask questions before then. During those earlier years, don't pull them aside for a serious talk or give a lecture or even bring up the subject often. Instead, be ready to respond when opportunities present themselves. For example, the birth of a baby in a friend's family might elicit the question, "Where do babies come from?" Or a TV ad or news story might provoke other comments and questions.

Younger children can be very open and frank about their thoughts. They might say, for example, "What are they doing in bed?" or "What does *sex* mean?" or "What's a condom?" When that happens, don't get flustered or embarrassed, and be sure to keep your answers positive. And don't unload everything at once. Eventually you need to let your children know that sex was God's idea and that it began at creation. You should also let them understand the purpose for sex (procreation, expression of love, pleasure) and that sex should be reserved for marriage.

As kids near adolescence, alert them to the physical and emotional changes they will experience. Then, as they become more aware of the opposite sex and sexual feelings, you can prepare them for the pressures and temptations they will face by explaining how people have differing values and lifestyles, alerting them about cultural myths, and warning them about potential problems and the effects of pornography, abuse, STDs and so forth. Again, in all of this be sure to focus on God's good (perfect) creation of sex—which is vastly different from what we see and hear these days.

In any case, don't worry about putting ideas in their heads. They'll get plenty of those from everyone else.

Dave Veerman

31. My kids think I'm old-fashioned in my views regarding sex and marriage. While I am a Christian and do believe that sex should be reserved for marriage, how can I convince my teenagers that I'm not just being a prude?

Whether or not they use the expression "old-fashioned," let your kids know that sometimes it's okay to hold on to things that are old, that were made or taught a long time ago. We can understand why all of us, especially the young, want to forget or discard the past, grasp the present and move into the future. Teenagers have been alive for just a short time (less that twenty years!), so they lack the adult perspective that comes with age and experience. And in many areas, especially technology and medicine, modern methods, machines and miracle drugs have improved our lives. For example, most of us can't imagine living without computers and cell phones, and returning to primitive transportation would be unthinkable. So it's easy to assume that "new" is always improved. But many things increase in value with age (for example, antiques and certain foods), and the truth never goes out of date. Gravity is old, but hey, it's the law! In fact, we live in a "constitutional democracy," and the Constitution was written more than two hundred years ago. Thus, when an idea or philosophy is presented, the most important question should be, "Is it true?" not "Is it new?"

Having said all that, you can point out that God and his Word never go out of date. Then, when it comes to sex, you can explain how God invented sex. It was his idea. Read Genesis 1:26—2:25 together and show how God pronounced his creation, including sex, "good." Adam and Eve had sex before sin entered the world. God also instituted marriage at that time. And God's perfect plan for sex—the best sex—is for it to be enjoyed by married couples (a man and a woman who have pledged themselves to each other for life). God knows what is best for us, and he wants only the best for us. It only makes sense, therefore, to live his way according to his rules and guidelines.

Encourage your kids to trust God and to trust you. And help them find positive role models. Explain that you know that this way of life, the choice to reserve sex for marriage, will be different, but they can "rebel" and do what is right and good and honoring to their Creator.

Dave Veerman

32. *Our sixteen-year-old daughter is seeing a seventeen-year-old boy whom we don't trust. Actually, we know very little about him, but we are reasonably certain that his values are not those shared by our family. He has multiple body piercings, wears gang-style clothing and has several tattoos on his neck and arms. When we told our daughter that we preferred she not date this particular young man, she got very angry with us. She says she's done nothing wrong and that we have no right to interfere in her relationships. We believe she is making a big mistake. Call it a parent's intuition or just plain common sense, but we are very worried about her. What should we do?*

Well, unless you have more evidence than you've presented here, you probably shouldn't draw too many conclusions about this young man based on his appearance. True, one's appearance often reveals something about his or her lifestyle and values, but keep in mind that most of today's kids just like to wear strange clothes and unusual body ornaments to differentiate themselves from their parents. Most of us did the same thing when we were young, although perhaps in not-so-extreme ways.

FIRST DATE

One of the rules when our two teenage daughters started dating was that the first date always had to be at our house for dinner. This was a good time for the boy to get to know us and for us to get to know him. We always had a good time. Today, our girls will tell you that there are some guys who they might have dated, but they knew better than to bring them home to meet us.

Jim Green

Your concern, however, is understandable. There's not a parent alive who doesn't worry to the point of panic when their daughters start going out with boys. Surely there's never been a boy in the history of the world good enough for our daughters.

So what action should you take? First, don't let fear, suspicion and anger dictate what you do. Negative emotions more often than not lead to dumb decisions. No one can fault you for wanting to protect your daughter from Jack the Ripper, but the only way you can protect her is to restrict her from seeing this young man, and she's made it clear that she won't allow you to do that. So if you restrict, she's bound to rebel, and that's certainly when your fears will become realized.

Your daughter is right. She hasn't done anything wrong. And she's also right that she is the only one who can decide who she "sees" or doesn't "see." At this point, all you can do is trust her. The best thing to do is admit that you overreacted and apologize for jumping to conclusions about her boyfriend. Let your daughter know that you believe in her and her ability to make responsible decisions. Remember, trust breeds trustworthiness.

The next step is to begin including the young man in your family activities. Invite him to be a regular guest at dinner. Request his presence at family outings. Be as welcoming to him as you possibly can. If he's the jerk that you suspect him to be, he will probably feel extremely uncomfortable around your family, in which case he's likely to quickly back out of your daughter's life. If he's not such a jerk, then your family's values can have nothing but a positive influence on him. He may just turn out to be the son-in-law of your dreams.

Wayne Rice

33. *I worry that my daughter is sexually active, but I'm not sure. Is there any way to find out without making her feel that I don't trust her?*

It's so encouraging to hear you ask this question. It shows that you really care about your daughter, and you are so right about the value of trust between a parent and teenager. Most kids realize how precious trust is and work hard to protect it. As they get older and move toward greater independence, they want to know that their parents respect the decisions they are making.

If they think that trust has been lost, some kids will hopelessly conclude that there is no point in living sensibly anymore: "They don't trust me anyway." When our kids live in a way that builds trust we need to let them know that we are noticing and that we like what we see.

You say you worry that your daughter is sexually active. I understand! With all the statistics we read these days it's hard not to worry. But don't assume that just because she's a teenager she's sexually active. There are growing numbers of kids who are choosing to remain sexually pure, and thankfully they can find friends who will support them in that decision. We need to be careful to base our level of trust on what we see in our individual sons and daughters rather than on national doom-and-gloom statistics.

There are some things that can be helpful in determining where our kids are at in terms of their sexual behaviors. The first and most important is (drum roll, please) just talk about it. Why is this often the last thing we consider? Assuming that you've kept the conversation going with your daughter since she was much younger, this is just a natural continuation of that discussion. Granted, as our kids get older the topics can get a little scarier, but I think we disappoint them when we shy away from the tough issues that they are dealing with. Avoid an accusing or assuming tone—which will immediately lead to defensiveness—but talk candidly about the value of wise sexual decision making and ask how they're doing in this area. As your kids get into dating relationships, promise them that you will hold them accountable in this area by asking the tough questions.

Listen carefully to the kinds of questions your daughter is asking. "Did you and dad have sex before you were married?" "Why are people so uptight about kids experimenting just a bit?" "How can you tell if you're really in love?" They are often an indication that important moral decisions are being made and can open the door to great discussions.

There are some legitimate danger signs you can watch for, and an involved parent will be sensitive to these: evasiveness about where she's going and with whom; sneaking out of the house late at night; spending long unsupervised hours at her boyfriend's house; an inappropriate level of physical affection when they are in public. While none of these are sure signs of sexual activity, they do represent a legitimate reason for a frank discussion about what's going on sexually.

Kids today are getting confusing messages about what is appropriate sexual behavior. As parents who care about our kids we need to be uncompromising in letting them know where we stand on these issues—never in an accusing or condescending way, but firmly, openly and lovingly. They need to know that it matters. Use the countless teachable moments that show up each day in the media and in the stories that come from their world to open conversations. Protect them from themselves by ensuring that they are not spending long hours in your home unsupervised; amazingly, the busiest hours for adolescent sexual activity are after school before parents get home from work.

One last thing. Try not to turn into the CIA. Sneaking around, spying on your kids, reading their private journals, polling their friends, tapping their phones and so on is usually relationally counterproductive. Develop the kind of rapport that will allow you to talk about these topics, and recognize that it's as important for your kids to trust you as it is for you to trust them.

Marv Penner

34. *What can we teach our son about masturbation? I think it's wrong, but I'd rather he do that than have sex and get a girl pregnant or something. I know I probably need to talk to him about it, but I'm not sure what to say.*

You say that you need to talk with him—that's the right attitude. Most parents shy away from talking to their kids about any sexual subject, especially this one. So talking with him at all is the biggest step.

Masturbation is a very difficult topic to tackle because it's so personal and, seemingly, so unavoidable. Most counselors and other experts agree that nearly 100 percent of boys masturbate. While that makes it normal, it doesn't necessarily make it a good habit to form. Masturbation may not be a sin (the Bible doesn't address the issue directly), but it's safe to say that it's not something most people like to admit they do a lot. It's less than the best.

When you talk with your son, explain that some sort of sexual release is natural. He's probably had wet dreams and may be confused about the experience. Wet dreams are natural, normal and often uncontrollable. But then explain that masturbation is different, mainly because it's something you choose to do, and it is usually accompanied by something that the Bible does identify as a sin: lust (Proverbs 6:25; Colossians 3:5). Explain how pornography plays into this and how some boys and men plan for masturbation, even keeping a stash of dirty pictures that they use for stimulation. Explain that the problem with porn, lust, X-rated movies, dirty jokes and so forth is that they treat women as sexual objects. Instead, we should see them as special creations of our loving God, just as we see ourselves.

Masturbation is not likely to reduce the odds of your son having sex or getting a girl pregnant. The only thing that will do that is a strong value system and a commitment by your son to remain sexually pure until marriage. You can help your son by teaching him the truth as you know it and by encouraging him in his walk with the Lord.

Dave Veerman

35. My fifteen-year-old daughter informed me that she is sexually active. I'm debating whether or not to provide her with birth control pills. Should I?

This has been an age-old question. Do I help my child do something wrong if they're going to do it anyway? "My son likes to shoplift. I can't seem to get him to stop. Do you think it would be a good idea for me to teach him some shoplifting skills so he doesn't get caught

lar satisfy their curiosity is to seek out information, often in the form of pornography. As you probably know, pornography is not difficult for them to find these days. If they can't find print or video pornography, it's available on the Internet and sometimes on prime-time TV!

The best way to deal with sexuality is to talk about it as honestly and openly as you know how. This is a great time for dad and son to talk. Consider this a teachable moment. Why not have a family night (or a dad and son time) once a week or once a month where you all discuss controversial subjects, using a question and answer approach. Sexuality is meant to be discussed in our homes, not just in the locker rooms at school. Create a safe place to discuss all the issues regarding sexuality, including pornography, homosexuality, masturbation, same-sex marriage, adultery and oral sex. Our kids have access to a lot more information than we think and certainly know a lot more than we did when we were their age!

The second issue is a teenager's right to privacy. It should also be no surprise to you that most parents have snooped in their teenagers' bedrooms. We have dealt with the issue of privacy elsewhere in this book, but suffice it to say that every parent has to determine their own ethics and policies regarding this issue. Personally, I am not in favor of snooping in a teenager's belongings unless there is some evidence of danger for your child or someone else (drugs, firearms, etc). Teenagers do need to feel that they have some private space, just as you do. But if you do believe that you have a right to enter your son's bedroom without a search warrant, make sure he understands this ahead of time, not after the fact.

If you feel you have violated your son's privacy, you may need to confess and apologize. Expect that there will be some fallout for some time, and don't get angry because your son is angry. You would be too. But you may choose instead to say nothing about the "found" por-

and go to jail?" or, "My teenager insists on playing on the busy freeway. He says it's real exciting. Should I buy him a helmet in case he gets hit by a speeding car or truck?"

If you believe that sex before marriage is wrong (and I hope you do), then talk with your daughter about that. This is the time for her to hear you say, "Darling, I cannot help you do something that will affect the rest of your life. I want you to be happy. I want you to enjoy sex for all of your life, not just now. The best way for that to happen is for you to someday be in a committed arrangement called marriage." You can either let your daughter know where you stand and what you believe is right, or you can sit by and let her continue in a path that is immoral, unhealthy, irresponsible, always risky and often the road to disease and unhappiness.

Do whatever it takes to protect her. This will not happen by putting locks on her bedroom door. It means building a new relationship built on openness, affection and, at times, tough love, sticking to your abstinence guns.

This may be the time to examine why your daughter feels a need to have sex with her boyfriend. A lot of sexually active teenagers come from homes where there isn't much affection, where parents are too busy with their own lives to provide that. Many teen girls get involved sexually with boys because they are seeking intimacy. They have a desire to be held, to be loved, to be desired. Very few girls seek sex for the sake of having sex. That's why fathers especially need to express love to their daughters by being involved in their lives and being appropriately affectionate. Your daughter needs to feel cherished and adored by dad.

Some teens use sex as a form of rebellion. Maybe they want to get back at their parents by getting pregnant or by saying, "If you don't care about me, I'll find someone who cares."

Talk to your daughter about all the issues. Communication is better than contraception. Before she continues being sexually active, she needs to decide if having sex before marriage is a wise choice.

Your daughter needs to know the real risk of sexually transmitted diseases (STDs). The probability for contracting a disease multiplies enormously for people who engage in promiscuous sex. Basically when you have sex with a person, you are having sex with everyone they've had sex with. Using the pill or a condom does not prevent being infected by a sexually transmitted disease.

And there's no foolproof way to avoid a pregnancy. Your daughter needs to know that if she becomes pregnant she'll have four choices, all very difficult.

- Raise the baby herself. Eighty percent of mothers who do this end up living in poverty for the rest of their lives.

- Put the baby up for adoption—and spend a lifetime wondering what's happening with your child. Yet, last year 2 million loving family adoption requests were unfulfilled.

- Have an abortion. I hope and pray this doesn't happen both for moral and psychological reasons.

- Get married to the boy. Having to get married is never a good way to start. If the boy doesn't want to get married, he is still legally and financially responsible for his child all the way through college.

Remember that it's never in our children's best interests to rescue them from consequences, but rather, to make sure they understand that they have the power to make wise choices and to determine the kind of life they want to live. Providing birth control pills is not the best way to teach responsibility to your daughter. She needs to learn responsibility on her own.

Jim Green

36. *We found pornography in our fifteen-year-old son's bedroom. aren't sure how to handle this situation. For one thing, we kn he'll be angry when he discovers that we were snooping aroun his things. Any suggestions?*

You raise two issues: pornography and privacy. Let's take the por raphy issue first. It should come as no surprise to you that at ag teen, your son has become a sexual being. God created us that There is heightened curiosity about sex from the time we enter m school (or for some, earlier!). One of the ways young men in pa

PORNOGRAPHY IS EVERYWHERE

One of my professors told his class about the time his middle-school son had a Playboy magazi hiding in his room. Somehow, the magazine was discovered. The boy was embarrassed, but Da dad) said, "Let's discuss what is being portrayed here." Dan said, "I never want you to feel th cannot talk about this stuff with me." This opened a door for Dan and his son to discuss sexual such as dating, abstinence, purity, "how far is too far" and how to handle lust.

Pornography is everywhere. There were 260 million pages of porn online, an increase of 1800 since 1998. Porn amounts to about 7 percent of the 3.3 billion pages indexed by Google. Bo to be tempted by this more than girls. Recent studies suggest a correlation between heighte aggressiveness in boys and exposure to pornography. Some studies state that young boys sti by pornography may become sexual abusers in adulthood.

My former professor was breaking the sexual code of "silence" by talking about it! Joshua Not Even a Hint (Multnomah) is an easy-to-read, practical and biblical book for young peop guarding against lust. For those with a son, I would encourage you to read with him Prepa Son for Every Man's Battle by Stephen Arterburn and Fred Stoeker (WaterBrook Press). They that attraction to the opposite sex is natural, that sex within marriage is exhilarating, tha slippery slope and that God has standards for sexual behavior. Discuss with your son the pc positive and negative) of sexual temptation, the way in which guys are drawn into sexua (the eye), and ways to protect the heart and mind. Your son needs to be encouraged to w and in the words of the book, it is "every young man's battle."

David Olshine

nography and wait for a teachable moment in which you bring up the subject and discuss it with him. If you have confiscated the pornography from your son's room, he will probably figure things out pretty fast anyway and bring it up himself. Expect some more fallout here. Whatever option you choose, honesty is always the best policy.

David Olshine

37. *I worry about my daughter. She is only eleven, but she is developing early and she already seems interested in boys. What can her mother and I do to make sure she doesn't become promiscuous with boys?*

Most teenage girls become intimate with boys not for physical reasons but for emotional ones. The best protection against promiscuous behavior is to give your daughter enough love and affection at home that she'll be less likely to seek it outside the home.

It is especially important for fathers to provide a good portion of that love and affection for their daughters. Much has been written about the important relationship between fathers and sons, but equally important is the relationship that fathers have with their daughters. Here are some tips:

- Give your daughter lots of attention. Prioritize your schedule so that you don't miss out on her activities. Take her out to lunch once in a while and go on a father-daughter "date" at a restaurant or to a movie. Let her know by your actions that she is loved and valued by the first man in her life.

- Say nice things to your daughter whenever you have the opportunity. Tell her that you love her. Tell her she's pretty. Write "love letters" to her. Girls who never hear words of affection and admiration from their dads are extremely vulnerable to boys who begin to notice how attractive they are.

- Talk to your daughter about relationships with boys. Give her insights into dating and relationships from a man's perspective. The more she knows about how boys think and behave, the better she'll be able to judge others and make wise decisions about her own behavior.

- Model good behavior in front of your daughter. Be romantic and respectful around your wife and demonstrate for your daughter what she should expect from any man who truly has her best interests in mind.

- Teach your daughter both by your example and by your instruction that sex appeal and physical attractiveness are not the most desirable traits in women, despite what the popular media would have her believe. Let her know that inner beauty is much more important than the shape of her body or the clothes she wears. Again, let her know that she is beautiful just the way she is.

- Have reasonable rules for her behavior and enforce them. Be clear about dating and curfew rules and the kinds of activities that she is allowed to participate in. Don't be afraid to set limits. Most teenagers privately wish their parents cared enough to enforce rules that are designed to protect them.

- Encourage her involvement in a church youth ministry. There are many reasons for this, but the most important one is that she might discover how much God loves her. When she has a relationship with Christ, she will be less needy and less vulnerable to promiscuity. In addition, she will get further instruction on godly dating and behavior, and she'll be more likely to meet other teens (including boys) who share those values.

Wayne Rice

38. *I brought up the subject of sex with my son and he just rolled his eyes at me, like he already knew everything. How can I convince my son that it's important for us to talk about sex?*

Don't try to convince your son that talking about sex is important; instead, just talk. And don't have this discussion in your home. You could go for a walk or a run together, have breakfast or lunch at a nearby restaurant, or go fishing. The talk can be short or long; the idea is to get away from the normal family environment and routine.

Begin by asking what other kids are thinking or saying. You could bring up, for example, a recent news item (sex-related) or popular movie and ask what his friends have said. The next step is to ask for his opinion. Be prepared to listen, intently and sincerely. In other words, don't simply wait for your turn to talk and then argue with what he says or launch into a lecture. Eventually, you will be able to share your information and ideas about sex. Even if you don't think you're getting through, just making the effort is important. Your son will know that he can talk with you about anything.

Dave Veerman

39. *I want to talk to my teenager about sexually transmitted diseases, but I really don't know what to say. I've read some literature, but I want to give my teenager the truth, not a lot of conservative propaganda. How can I sort out the facts from fiction?*

Most kids wish they had a parent who wasn't squeamish about these topics. A lot of us assume that our teens have all the information they need on important sexual issues, but it's just not necessarily so. As sophisticated as today's kids seem to be, there's still much they need to hear from their parents when it comes to understanding the implications of their sexual choices.

You're quite right to be concerned about the flavor of propaganda present in a lot of the written material on adolescent sexuality—everyone seems to have their own view of morality, and it's reflected in the way each group's information is communicated. Frankly, I'd be just as worried about the liberal propaganda from the pro-anything-goes crowd as I am with the conservative stuff you express concern about. My personal feeling is that if I'm going to err about something that could kill my kid, I'd rather err on the side of caution. The secret is to find the facts and then present those to your son or daughter on the basis of the relationship you have with them.

The good news is that because you're asking about a topic that is objectively medical and scientific, there is verifiable truth to be found. Look to medical sources that aren't driven by a special-interest group and read as widely as you can. Talk to your family doctor, who will be able to guide you to unbiased medical information. Don't be afraid to buy a book that deals frankly with adolescent sexuality and make it available to your teenager. Just don't use the old "book left on the night table" trick as an excuse not to talk about it.

As you probably know, one of the major problems in dealing with teenagers is their sense of immortality: "It would never happen to me." Of all the misunderstandings around STDs this is probably the one that needs to be addressed most aggressively. No matter how "careful" they might be during sexual encounters, they are never in-vulnerable to STDs, and they need to be reminded of it. In addition, they need to understand that although symptoms of some STDs can be suppressed, the disease itself may remain present for many years, putting them and their eventual marriage partner in jeopardy. This is a serious topic with huge long-term implications.

In reality, the only way for a teenager to guarantee an STD-free body is to remain abstinent.

When you talk to your teenager about this crucial topic there are a few things to keep in mind. Don't assume that your teenager is sexually active or has immediate plans to become so. On the other hand, don't be naive either. Avoid a spirit of paranoia or panic in your discussion of these topics. It might cause your teenager to become even more casual about it just to balance your anxiety. Ask what they are learning about STDs in school and then measure it against the information you are finding. This can create a great basis for conversation. The bottom line is to keep talking about these subjects even though it feels a bit awkward.

Marv Penner

40. *I hate to admit this, but I worry constantly that my teenager might become a homosexual. He hasn't really done anything to make me think that's happening, but I still worry about it. Is this normal?*

Homosexuality is much more accepted in our culture these days, and our kids are being exposed to the homosexual lifestyle constantly. For this reason alone, you shouldn't be embarrassed that you worry about the impact of all this on your teenager and the choices that he must make regarding his sexuality as he gets older. Further, worry is perfectly normal for parents, whether it's about kids driving home late at night, using drugs, failing classes at school or experimenting with "alternative" lifestyles.

People today hold many different views about homosexuality. Most Christians hold to the traditional view that homosexuality is forbidden by Scripture and therefore a sinful, deviant form of sexuality (Romans 1:18-25). Others believe that homosexuality is not a choice at all, but part of a person's genetic code, determined before birth. Some differentiate between homosexual feelings and homosexual behavior. Regardless of your view, there's no question that this is an emotional issue that can be extremely volatile for families and everyone involved.

Why do you worry so much about this? Is your son not dating? Does he seem uninterested in the opposite sex? Does he hang out exclusively with guys? Does he have some personality traits that don't seem "masculine"? Though these might be reason for concern, in and of themselves none of these are conclusive predictors of homosexuality. In fact, all of these things are relatively normal for adolescent boys.

BY CHOICE OR BY CHANCE?

Is homosexuality something you are born with?

Some say yes, some say no. There are strong arguments that can be made to support both sides of this issue.

But some believe the answer is somewhere in the middle. Rather than arguing that everyone is born with a particular sexual orientation, this view holds that everyone is born with personality traits that make them more or less inclined toward homosexuality. In other words, just as some people are born left-handed rather than right-handed, some are born to be more open to the homosexual lifestyle than others. That doesn't mean they are born homosexuals; it just means that homosexuality is an easier choice for them to make.

It's safe to say that everyone has a desire and a need for intimacy with others of the same sex. There's nothing wrong with that. Young men need to feel loved by other men, especially their fathers. Young women also have a great need to be close to other women, especially their mothers. When these natural desires for intimacy are sexualized, they become perverted and result in unhealthy relationships that are rarely fulfilling.

We can help young people make good choices by providing them with healthy role models, both male and female. Boys need to be around men who will affirm them and show them what it means to be a godly man. Girls also need to have women in their lives who will teach them how to become godly women. Parents are primary, of course, but youth also need mentors outside the home. When they are deprived of healthy same-sex relationships, they may seek them in unhealthy ways.

Wayne Rice

If your teen has strong homosexual feelings or is predisposed toward homosexuality, he probably will not come out and tell you. The phrase "coming out of the closet" indicates that there is a great deal of fear and anxiety associated with the admission of homosexual feelings. Even though homosexuality is accepted in some places, it is not accepted everywhere. To admit to homosexuality is to risk rejection and judgment from others, including those who are members of your own family.

Communication is vital if the worry continues to plague you. I am not suggesting that you come right out and ask him, "Are you struggling with homosexuality?" but rather say, "If there are some fears you'd like to talk about, I am here to listen." This approach opens the door for dialogue, and if he chooses it, you'll have a chance to offer guidance and support. At our Understanding Your Teenager seminars, we teach that the older a teenager gets, the less controlling we are to be as parents. This applies to every aspect of life. Let your son know that there are no taboo subjects and that even though it may be unsettling, you will do your best to coach when needed, consult when wanted, and most of all, you will always love and care for him no matter what the issue is about.

One marker that might lead you to explore the issue more with your son is his emotional condition. If he is struggling with homosexuality, he will probably experience periods of guilt and depression. If you notice these emotions in your son, you may want to get him some help. Until then, stop worrying. The Bible encourages us not to worry but to give our fears to God. Jesus said, "Give your entire attention to what God is doing right now, and don't get worked up about what may or may not happen tomorrow. God will help you deal with whatever hard things come up when the time comes" (Matthew 6:33-34 *The Message*). That is encouraging for all parents who have the "gift" of anxiety—cast your worries on God and he will help you deal with whatever hard things come up, if and when they do.

Meanwhile, don't treat your son as if he were a homosexual. Statistically speaking, it's unlikely that he is. Avoid making fun of lesbians or homosexuals. Don't reinforce stereotypes or engage in "gay bashing." Stay connected with your son; keep on loving him, praying for him and being the strong role model that he needs in his life right now.

David Olshine

41. I found birth control pills in my daughter's handbag. What should I do?

What makes parenting so tough is that it brings together two vivid realities: (a) the massive investment of our love and concern in kids who, (b) as they grow older, grow increasingly beyond the range of our ability to protect that investment. It is a grand and glorious risk. But it also helps to explain our deep fear and disappointment when we have an experience like the one you've had. It's a mixture of grief, betrayal, fear, anger and concern. And there is no one right, surefire response in this situation.

What I can say for sure is this: you must talk to your daughter about this. And you must do it right away.

- Don't wait for just the right moment. It may not come. Obviously, this is not a conversation to have just before you drop her off at the church for youth group. But don't keep hoping this will come up comfortably. It will not. Break the no-talk rule before it breaks something precious for you and your daughter.

- Don't be too quick to accept what your daughter knows you want to hear: "The pills are for a friend," "They're for a science experiment," "I thought they were breath mints." This is not the time for wishful thinking.

- Don't allow the conversation to get sidetracked. If your daughter is like 95 percent of other teenagers, she will try to shift the focus of the offense from sexual promiscuity to invasion of privacy: "I can't believe you were spying on me, and going through my things!" You found what you found, and that is the issue at hand.

- Don't let this end your relationship with your child. Before you have this conversation, go back and read Luke 15:11-20. Notice very carefully two facets of the story. First, the father understood that some children can only truly come home if we truly let them leave. As painful as it is, we cannot protect them from every pain and consequence. And second, remember that the father extended love to his son "while he was still a long way off," well before he knew that the son had decided to turn his life around.

- Do not allow your sense of grief and betrayal to trump your unconditional love. Your daughter needs you now more than ever. If you push her aside and physically or emotionally distance yourself from her you will be driving her toward the worst possible choices.

The hardest issue? Where you go after the crying and the conversation is over.

Approach one. There are those who point out the studies that show how powerful parental opinions are in shaping the moral choices of adolescents. And based on that line of reasoning, they would be against allowing your daughter to keep taking the pill, because your explicit permission to use the pills might communicate implicit approval of her sexual behavior.

Approach two. There are others who would counsel that a child who carries birth control pills in her purse is sexually active, and whether or not you approve of her behavior, she should be supported in using the pill if she's going to be sexually active. Better to be a mother to a sexually active teenager than a grandmother with a sexually active teenage mother.

Frankly I don't think it's possible for anyone but the parents to answer that question because the answer would vary from child to child. To be sure, I would lean very strongly to approach number one. In my years of youth ministry experience, and based on what I know of studies on adolescent behavior, I would not want to underestimate the potency of parental influence. Any movement in the direction of approach number two would come only after considerations of age and attitude. If I were convinced that this child had moved beyond a place of parental influence, or if, in fact, she was at an age that placed her beyond parental control, then I might reluctantly—with clearly stated reservations and with much prayer—opt for approach number two.

Duffy Robbins

42. *Last week our fourteen-year-old daughter was invited to go out with a boy on a date. While we know the boy and we also know that the activity is going to be chaperoned, we still don't think our daughter is old enough to start dating. What do you think? When is it appropriate for teenagers to start dating?*

Here's the quick answer to your question: "Yes, fourteen is too young and sixteen is just about right." But quick answers tend to be unsatisfying, so here are some additional thoughts.

First, the pressure to date is real and very strong, especially in some groups within the school. Your daughter probably wants to be popular (who doesn't!) and would like to have an active social life.

She may even be interested in the boy who asked her out. So, quite naturally, she would like to date, and date him in particular. But dating at a young age isn't a good idea. It puts the couple, especially the girl, under even more pressure and in the middle of boy-girl intrigues. Note that often the older boys are the ones who want to date the younger girls, which opens another can of worms. By waiting till sixteen, your daughter will still have a couple of years to date in high school.

Saying no to your daughter won't be easy, and she probably won't like your answer or attitude. But this takes the pressure off her. You might even say something like this: "Tell your friends that your mean, old and strict parents won't let you." In other words, you be the bad guy in the situation. Some parents are so worried about what other parents and their teenagers think of them that they don't do what they should with their own kids. Don't

LICENSED TO DATE

Think of dating like driving. Teens aren't automatically ready to drive when they turn sixteen; they need to take a driver's education class, receive behind-the-wheel instruction, obtain a learner's permit, and pass the written test and the actual driving test. There is a lot of preparation that goes into learning how to drive.

Why?

Because it's potentially very dangerous.

The same is true for dating. In fact, in some cases, dating could be more hazardous to your teen's health than driving.

What's a parent to do?

Spend as much time preparing your teens to date as you spend training them to drive. Don't assume that your children will be ready to date when they are sixteen any more than you would expect them to be ready to drive just because they are sixteen. They might be ready to date when they are fourteen, but they might not be ready even when they are eighteen. Age is not as important as maturity and readiness.

Teens are ready to date when they know the benefits of dating, the dangers of dating, and have personal standards for dating, just like they are ready to drive when they know the benefits and dangers of driving, and know the rules of the road and are willing to follow them.

Tim Smith

make this a battle. Simply explain your decision and reasons to your daughter without losing your cool, even if she responds with a teenage tantrum.

During this discussion or at another more teachable moment, talk through the purpose of dating. At that time you can tell your daughter that you're not against boys and that you want her to get to know members of the opposite sex. Then you can talk about how to do that outside of one-on-one dates and how casual, informal opportunities are even better than dating.

Every teenager is unique, so you may have a very mature fourteen-year-old, and you probably know some very immature sixteen-year-olds. We don't want to belittle our kids and talk down to them or think the worst of our kids and accuse. At the same time, however, we don't do our children any favors by assuming a maturity level that isn't there. Physically mature young people are often assumed to be mature in other areas as well. A freshman girl may look like a senior but probably is still fourteen emotionally. Conversely, just because a boy or girl turns sixteen doesn't mean that he or she is ready to date. (They may not want to anyway.) Sometimes the pressure to date comes from the parents.

During the couple of years before that sixteenth birthday, you may find exceptions to your rule or situations in which you can compromise—the event is more like a group date, you know the boy and his family well, it's a church youth group banquet, and so forth.

Dave Veerman

---

43. When I was a teenager, I made a lot of mistakes. For example, I got pregnant and had an abortion which I now regret. I don't want my daughter to make the same mistakes I made, but who am I to give her advice? I don't feel like I have any credibility with her.

If only it was that simple: live a regret-free adolescence and have instant credibility with your kids. Blow it when you are a teenager and watch your own kids go down the same path.

Fortunately, most kids are a lot smarter than that. Your credibility with your daughter is based on the kind of relationship you've developed with her in the years you've spent together, not on what happened before she was born. What kids are looking for in a parent is honesty and relational involvement, not perfection.

Actually, there may be no one in a better position to speak about the very real dangers surrounding tough sexual choices than you are. You obviously understand some of the outcomes in a way that others can only theorize about. What your daughter needs from you is a willingness to frankly discuss things with her as it becomes appropriate or as she asks.

There are a few things you may want to keep in mind as you consider what parts of your experiences to share. Don't assume that your daughter wants (or needs) to hear every detail of your story. When it comes to our past it's easy to err on either side of balance. We can tell too little because of the shame we feel and the fear that honesty will destroy parental credibility, or we can tell too much for the sake of venting all of the pent-up emotions around our story. The challenge will be to filter your decisions through your understanding of your daughter's needs rather than your own. Ask yourself what will be most helpful to her, and keep her age and relational maturity in mind as you decide what you'll tell her.

Given what you've said about your own story, I'm sure you've already realized that it will be easy to become overcautious in your parenting. You know how quickly you can blow it as a teenager, and you also understand how serious the consequences can be. Take a deep breath and relax. Your past can actually prepare you to have a healthy basis for discussion instead of setting you up to be a paranoid "dating cop."

Just one more thing. It sounds as though there may still be some unresolved issues around some of your own pain from the past. It might be helpful for you to find a pastor or counselor who can help you think through issues of forgiveness and grace in your own life. As long as fear, guilt and shame are the primary emotions you feel when you think about your past, you can be sure that they will shape your relationships with the people around you. It will be important to work that stuff out with someone other than your daughter—that way you can be free to be the caring, healthy mom it sounds like you want to be.

Marv Penner

44. We just found out our sixteen-year-old is pregnant. The father is a young man who we definitely do not want her to marry. We don't believe in abortion, so what are our options? What should we do?

It's time to circle the wagons. This is not a situation for you to have to handle alone.

Your first step should be to create a support team for yourself and your daughter. I would start with Mercy Ministries (<http://www.mercyministries.com>, P.O. Box 111060, Nashville, TN 37222-1060, (615) 831-6987, info@mercyministries.com) and get a little coaching from the folks who have dealt with this same situation thousands of times. You might also call your local crisis pregnancy center. You can find information about resources nearest you from CareNet (800-395-4357).

Next, make sure your own oxygen mask is in place. Remember the airline safety instructions: "If you are traveling with someone in need of assistance, place the oxygen mask on yourself before trying to assist others." You will be of little support to your daughter if you are perpetually anxious and overwhelmed by her situation. So whether it is a support group of peers, family members, a pastor or a counselor, make sure that you stay well connected to an extended family that can give you the support you need as you walk through these crisis months.

Of course, your daughter will need lots of support through this process. This is a time for listening. Pressure, rejection, threats, accusations will do little to help her move in a positive direction. You have the chance here to model the unconditional love of God for her (and the rest of your family). Whatever the outcome, she (and her child) have a better chance of thriving in the future if you stay connected. It is particularly important that, as much as possible, her father takes time to assure her that she is still deeply loved by him.

This may be a time when she wants only to talk to her friends for support. But she will need much more than the inexperienced advice of her peers. Hopefully she has friendships with some adults outside your home—a youth pastor, a teacher, a youth leader whom you respect. If not, it will be important for you to help her "stack the stands" for herself, to surround herself with loving adults who will let her know that in spite of her situation, she is cherished by God. If she had previously made a commitment to abstinence, she may feel particularly ashamed and disappointed in herself. Help her bring that guilt to God and ask for forgiveness.

You will certainly want to be selective about deciding who learns about her situation and when, but total secrecy will only add an extra burden to her that will do little to clarify the decision-making process. More importantly, making secrecy a priority will limit your freedom to surround yourself and your daughter with the kind of support she desperately needs.

As far as the boy is concerned, your best hope is to provide your daughter the kind of loving, nonreactive support I have just suggested. If you spend a lot of anxious energy talking negatively about this relationship, you may, in fact, push your daughter more deeply into it.

Mark DeVries

FRIENDS

45. *How can we get our teenager to stop hanging out with the group of losers he considers his friends? We've tried to convince him that these kids will only drag him down, but he just gets mad at us and refuses to listen.*

First of all, if your son hears you refer to his friends as losers, you shouldn't be surprised by his anger. Teenagers take attacks on their friends very personally. If you try to alienate your son from his friends—whether or not they are "losers"—you will more than likely alienate your son from you.

But you do have a right to be concerned. Scripture teaches that "bad company corrupts good character" (1 Corinthians 15:33), a principle that we've all learned the hard way. We know how dangerous negative peer pressure can be.

What makes you think of your son's friends as losers? Is it their appearance? Are they not Christians? Do they engage in immoral or illegal behavior? Try not to judge them based solely on your impressions or on "outward appearances." If you know that they are involved in activities that are harmful in some way, then you do have a right (and a duty) to intervene in the relationship. Good parents set limits and forbid their teenagers to spend time with individuals who are known to be involved in behaviors that are illegal, immoral or harmful. Notice, however, that such limits are based on behavior—not appearance, economic status, race or other prejudicial criteria.

What about your son? If he is a Christian and his friends are not, this gives him a great opportunity to influence them in a positive way. He can be light and salt to his friends. By living his faith, your son may be able to influence his friends and create a desire for them to know Jesus. The Lord Jesus himself was accused of hanging out with sinners. There's no real harm in doing that.

If your son is not firm in his faith, however, influence may run in the other direction. You'll want to monitor things and let your son know exactly what the limits and boundaries are. For example, if it is clear that his friends are pulling him away from church or family activities, you can create rules that govern these behaviors and enforce them with consequences.

If you would like to help your son find better friends, here are some things you can do. First, stop being so critical of him. Accept him for who and what he is. Your son's self-image is determined by what he sees in the most important mirror in his life—his parents. And when a teenager's self-image improves, so does his choice of friends.

Second, provide opportunities for your son to meet a variety of other teenagers, especially those who share your family's values and faith. Support your church's youth ministry. Encourage your son to go on a short-term mission or service project. The more he interacts with other young people who are not "losers," the more likely he'll be to make friends with them.

Third, get to know your son's friends a little better. Pray for them. You may be surprised to find out that they aren't such losers after all. And as a result of your prayer and mentoring in their lives, they may change . . . which would mean your son ends up with better friends!

Here's something else to think about. Most teenagers enter into lots of "trial and error" relationships during their adolescent years. They experiment with friendships—usually to find out more about themselves. They move from one group of friends to another until they find a group they can identify and feel comfortable with. Don't interfere with this process, but work with it. Treat your teenager respectfully, and he will more than likely end up with friends who also have a degree of self-respect.

If you're like most people, you probably made some pretty poor friendship choices when you were a teenager. If you survived them, there's a pretty good chance your son will do the same.

David Olshine

46. Our daughter has some friends who we know are having a bad influence on her. Every day we see changes . . . in her appearance, her attitude, her behavior. We have forbidden her to spend any more time with these people, but she does it anyway and lies to us. Now what should we do?

There are many reasons why teenagers choose the friends they do, but when it gets right down to it, adolescent friendships are all about being accepted, fitting in, feeling cared for and figuring out who you are. As kids begin the process of separating from family in their early adolescence, their need for a safe place to belong remains as strong as ever. Friends often become their "second family," and loyalty can be passionate.

Your concerns about the friends your daughter is choosing are legitimate and need to be addressed, but when it comes to this topic we are usually walking a pretty thin line. Forbidding a teenager from spending time with someone they see as an ally may just intensify their commitment to the friendship. Power struggles over friendships can end up creating the opposite reaction of what you are hoping for. It seems as though that's already happening with the lying and sneaking around you're seeing. These behaviors indicate a lack of respect that must be taken seriously.

The highest priority right now is rebuilding a relationship of mutual trust and respect with your daughter. It may take significant time and effort. You'll need to find some safe connecting points with her and look for creative ways to let her know you love her. She'll probably be defensive and resistant, but remember that most teenagers value their relationship with their parents even though they sometimes don't act that way.

Unfortunately, when kids surround themselves with negative friends it can be a reflection of how they see themselves. Instead of fighting with your daughter you might want to look for ways to help her feel better about herself. Help her get involved in sports, music or some sort of leadership role. When she begins to see herself as "out of their league" she will find them less attractive. In the meantime do what you can to make your home a happy place for her to bring her friends—it's always best to have the party at your house, even when you're not thrilled about some of the kids who are there.

If things continue to get worse, you may have to take more drastic steps—not by applying more pressure but by finding ways to remove your daughter from proximity to the people who are dragging her down. It may mean having her change schools or even a move to a new neighborhood if things get serious enough.

Marv Penner

47. I have no idea who my son's friends are. How can I find out?

It's not unusual for teenagers to keep their private lives to themselves.

We ask, "Where are you going?" and they answer, "Out." We ask, "Who are you going with?" and they say, "Nobody." This can be very frustrating to parents.

So what can you do? First, don't stop asking. If you get that "Nobody" response, ask again: "Okay, but could you tell me who Nobody is? Seriously, I'd like to know who your friends are. It's important to me." Try to do this in a way that invites a response. You don't want your interactions to come across as interrogations. This should be a conversation. And remember, no matter what they say, you must be careful not to react or respond negatively toward anyone they name. You can ask for more information, but keep it light and unthreatening.

While we're on the subject of conversation, keep in mind that any conversation will do. Just find some time to talk with your son. My guess is that—sooner or later—the subject of his friends will come up quite naturally. You won't have to pry the information out of him.

Maybe your primary concern is that he never brings them to your home. In that case, extend an invitation to them. Tell him you'd really like for him to invite his friends over. It's possible that there are reasons why he wouldn't want to do this—he might be embarrassed by his friends (or by you), or he may feel uncomfortable bringing them to his house for some reason. Explore these issues with him and suggest other ways you could host a get-together with his friends. If he agrees, do your best to be a good host—cordial and friendly.

The main issue here seems to be one of communication. You really need to open up the communication lines and work on the relationship you have with your son. Don't expect him to tell you everything that's going on in his life (including who all his friends are), but the better the relationship you have with him, the more he will let you into his private world.

Jim Green

48. I know that friends are very important to teenagers, but my son doesn't seem to have any. He's content to stay home most of the time and just entertain himself. Is this abnormal? What can I do to encourage him to be less of a loner and to find some friends?

Some people need friends more than others. A true extrovert, for example, thrives on relationships—life seems to revolve around being with others. An introvert, however, can be happy alone. Sometimes an extrovert parent has difficulty relating to a more introverted son or daughter and vice versa. So your son may be normal. You are right to say that friends are important to teenagers, but for some the need is more intense. Everyone, however, needs people who care. Certainly family can help meet that need.

If your son truly is lonely, help him brainstorm possible places to find friends. Use the acronym CIN. C stands for closeness: does he know of any potential friends in his classes or other activities? I stands for interests: Does he have a special interest (for example, music, computers, a hobby, a sport or so forth) that he would have in common with others? And N stands for need: Does he

SOCIAL INTELLIGENCE

Friends are terribly important to teens, but they don't always determine if the teen will have social intelligence—the skills and knowledge that brings relational effectiveness. A comprehensive study of teenagers found that one out of five teens suffers from alienation. In fact, most teens expect some level of rejection or alienation from their friends; it's seen as part of the teenage jungle. The encouraging news from this study is that, because most teens expect some rejection from friends, their home life has more to do with their levels of alienation than their social life.

That is good news. We can't always influence what happens at school with our teens and their friends; nor should we try! But we can influence what happens at home. Ask yourself the following questions:

■ Are we connecting with our teens?
■ Do we show interest in their friends and interests?
■ Do our teens feel valued?
■ Do we value family time enough to make it fun, relaxed and memorable?

Tim Smith

know another student who also needs a friend—perhaps someone new to the school? He can mine those three locations for potential friends.

The idea is not to push or pressure your son but to get him to think, to broaden his perspective and expand his options. And give him opportunities to meet potential friends: church youth group, Campus Life, Young Life, and so forth. There's no better place to find a good friend.

Dave Veerman

49. *My thirteen-year-old daughter hangs around with a negative group of kids her age. A couple of boys do drugs. Her girlfriends get into trouble in school. How can I help her avoid these types of friends?*

The issue of friends is a tough one because there's not a lot you can do to determine the outcome of your daughter's friendship choices. When she was little you could provide her with playmates. But now that she's older, playmates will no longer do. She needs friends, and she will most definitely choose her own.

With a thirteen-year-old, the first thing I would suggest is to be very clear with your daughter regarding any rules that you believe are important for her. You can't choose her friends, but you can put reasonable limits on her friendship choices. For example: "You are absolutely not allowed to hang out with people who use drugs, drink alcohol, or have a police record." If you know for a fact that certain boys are using drugs, then it's not only your right but your responsibility to forbid your daughter from spending time with them.

A word to the wise here: As teens get older, rules like these should become less necessary. It's generally best to avoid interfering with your teenager's choice of friends. Here's why:

- Teenagers can benefit from even the most ill-advised friendships. Sometimes the only way to learn how to choose good friends is to have a few bad ones along the way.

- When parents try to micromanage their teenagers' lives, the teen-agers rarely do better. Instead, they do worse. Picking your kid's friends is micromanaging at its worst.

- It's virtually impossible to force a teenager to have the friends you want them to have. When you try to force friendships on a teen-ager, the result is almost always rebellion.

- The only time you should interfere with a teenager's choice of friends is when there is a need to protect them from serious and imminent harm.

There is an old proverb that says "Birds of a feather flock together." This is true for teenagers as well. Most teens choose friends who they identify with in some way. They tend to gravitate toward other teens who they perceive are most like themselves.

In light of this, I would suggest that you avoid being overly critical and negative toward your daughter. Teens who have low self-esteem generally gravitate toward friends who also have low self-esteem and no self-respect. The more you are able to give your daughter a high view of herself, the less likely she will be to choose friends who will drag her down. Try to be positive and encouraging toward her. If you express faith in her ability to make good choices, she'll be more likely to make them.

On the other hand, if you are certain that your daughter has cho-sen friends who are using drugs or engaging in other behaviors that are harmful, this could be an indicator that your daughter is also in-volved. Don't be the last to find out. Investigate and monitor her be-havior closely. Be on the lookout for drug paraphernalia or changes in her attitude and speech. Talk with her about drugs and make sure she is in agreement that they should be avoided at all costs. If you suspect that there is a problem, don't hesitate to get help from a pro-fessional counselor or youth worker.

You may need to change her environment. I encourage parents to do whatever they can to make sure their kids have every opportunity to choose good friends. If you are able, make sure your daughter is in a good school that has strong adult leadership and high standards for behavior. Get her involved in a church youth group or Christian organization that gives her a greater chance of finding friends who share your family's values and beliefs. You can't choose her friends, but sometimes you can surround her with people who might become her friends.

Remember that it's normal for parents to worry about their teenagers' friends. Sometimes the worry is justified; quite often it's not. Most of us had some questionable friends when we were kids and we survived; chances are good that your daughter will too. If she is doing well at school, has strong moral and spiritual values, and is not engaging in any bad behaviors that you know of, don't assume the worst. It's almost impossible to protect our children from every kind of negative influence. Just because she has a few friends who are in trouble doesn't necessarily mean that she is also in trouble. But stay vigilant and involved. Talk with her about friends and share from your own experience. If you stay connected with your daughter and teach her right from wrong, there's a high probability that she will develop the strength of character to resist negative peer pressure.

Wayne Rice

50. *My twelve-year-old son has special needs and is in a public school. He is endeared by most, but is rarely invited to a friend's house or parties. We want him to be more independent and have peer friends. I'm sure it bothers us more than it does him, but we'd like to help. What should we do?*

It can be painful for any parent when their child is not embraced the way we had hoped for, and this is especially true with special-needs kids. It sounds like your son has adjusted well to the public school and the school to him. It is not surprising that your son is endeared by many. Children (and adults) with special needs are some of the most lovable and likeable people on the planet. Their innocence, love, compassion, sensitivity, humor and down-to-earth practical sense are reasons they are referred to as "special." I know because I am the parent of a special-needs child.

Be patient as you wait for other students to reach out to your son in friendship. It's not easy for "normal" youth to feel comfortable around special-needs kids. They sometimes compensate for their discomfort by ignoring kids with special needs or, worse, by being cruel—making fun of them or humiliating them publicly. This can be heartbreaking for us as parents, but it seems that God often provides a shield for our special-needs kids—they don't feel nearly as embarrassed or put down as we might in the same situation.

If your son doesn't seem to be bothered by the rejection that obviously concerns you, perhaps it's best to let a sleeping dog lie, as they say. Some teen parties are better off being avoided anyway. I would hate to hear that your son attended a party and some "bully" put drugs into his soft drink just to entertain himself or his friends.

It might be best for you to plan your own social events. Ask your son if he has friends from school he'd like to have over at the house or go with him to the football game. You can help him invite those friends and make all the arrangements. This way you are still in the socialization business plus you have a certain element of control.

As you said, your son is endeared by most—so it's likely that he will find some caring friends who will want to include him in some of their social activities. Not only will your son benefit, so will his friends.

David Olshine

BEHAVIOR AND DISCIPLINE

51. *Teenagers are too big to spank. So how can I effectively discipline my two kids without treating them like children?*

Teenagers are definitely too big and too mature to spank. That means that you must find alternate ways to make your children "uncomfortable." That is basically what discipline accomplishes. Discipline makes a child feel uncomfortable and then they (hopefully) try to avoid what has caused that uncomfortable feeling.

What are some things your children enjoy? Do they like having the freedom of being able to drive your car? Do they enjoy spending time on the Internet instant messaging their friends? What about using the telephone or having friends over? Whatever it is, if you connect that enjoyable experience with the limits you have set for your teenager, your teens will learn how to modify their behavior in order to protect the experiences they enjoy. Be sure to be reasonable and responsible with your discipline, establishing limits and consequences *before* the offense whenever possible.

Kendra Smiley

52. *What's the best way to monitor what our kids are doing? I sometimes have no idea what they are up to.*

The best way to learn your kids' schedules is to ask. Some parents are afraid to ask or think they won't get a respectful answer. If that's the way you feel, ask anyway. Sometimes our kids assume that our asking leads to judging, lecturing or worse. Husbands and wives often make that assumption in their relationship too. For example, the husband may ask, "What time is dinner?" And the wife will snap back, "I'm going as fast as I can!" (assuming a motive for his

THE GOAL OF DISCIPLINE

The goal of discipline is not to punish but to teach responsibility. Punishment more often than not leads to anger and resentment. Discipline, on the other hand, leads to an increase in self-discipline and self-esteem. Teenagers who are disciplined rather than punished learn that they are in control of their lives and that what they do matters.

The key to discipline is learning how to use consequences effectively. Consequences save parents from threatening, screaming, nagging or using physical violence of any kind. Consequences hold teenagers responsible for their actions.

Basically, there are two kinds of consequences. Natural consequences happen naturally. For example, if your teenager forgets to set his alarm clock, he's probably going to be late. Natural consequences work best when we don't interfere with them.

Logical consequences, however, don't happen naturally. They are created in advance, agreed on and understood by your teenager as what happens when certain behaviors are chosen. For example, if your teenager chooses to disobey curfew rules, she also chooses the consequence, which may adversely affect her going-out privileges. As the name implies, logical consequences must be logical (make sense) if they are going to be effective. Consequences should always be presented as choices, not threats.

We undermine discipline when we fail to be clear about consequences or fail to follow through on their implementation. Remember, consequences are tools with which we teach teenagers to be responsible and learn to make good choices. They are not punishment, and they will fail if they are presented as such.

Wayne Rice

AFTER SCHOOL

The hours immediately after school can be a dangerous time for teenagers. Researchers have found that there is an undeniable correlation between the amount of time teens are left unsupervised after school and the likelihood that they will drink alcohol, smoke cigarettes, do drugs, engage in sexual activity or become victims of violence.

For this reason alone, it is important for parents to monitor the whereabouts of their teens and to encourage them to participate in positive after-school activities or hobbies they might be interested in.

If your teen would rather not participate in a supervised after-school activity, don't force the issue. Some teens are perfectly fine being alone after school and would rather spend their time at home listening to music, talking on the phone, working on their homework or just sleeping. Older teens might be interested in an after-school job.

Talk (and listen) to your teenager and find out what he or she would like to do. He might say, "Don't worry, Mom. I just want to hang out at home and work on my car." In that case, you might help him round up some decent tools.

Just remember that it's important for you to stay involved and keep tabs on what your kids are doing. Set limits and be clear on any rules that you believe are important. Teens understand that parents have a need (and a right) to know what they are doing and will always do better when they know their parents care.

Tim Smith

question). So you may want to preface your question by pointing out that you're just gathering information. Don't snoop or badger your kids, questioning them about every minute of their lives. But let them know that you have a need to know what they're doing at certain times—evenings, parties, weekends and so forth. You are the parent, not a stranger, a neighbor or a buddy. You have the right, and responsibility, to know. This process will be easier if you share your schedule with them as well. Good communication works both ways.

Dave Veerman

53. *My teenager lies to me constantly. Even though I can't always prove that she's lying, I don't trust her anymore. How can I ever believe what she says?*

Every parent has to decide what issues to "go to the mat" over with their teenage children. You've probably heard the counsel "pick your battles wisely," so the first question you have to ask yourself is, *Is this something worth battling over?*

When it comes to lying, the answer is yes.

Right now your daughter lies for one simple reason: because it works. She has likely had enough "success" in lying to convince her that it is almost always worth the risk. She has learned that a well-placed lie can sometimes provide her with an almost magical, Houdini-like ability to slip out of sticky situations. And even if she does get caught in a lie, she has learned that the consequences are usually minimal compared to the potential gain of getting totally out of trouble.

Research into the behavior of today's teenagers has repeatedly revealed that the vast majority of teenagers admit to lying to their parents. So we shouldn't be surprised when our kids periodically lie to us. Acknowledging this fact does not excuse the lying, but it is a great motivation for every parent of a teenager to create a game plan for when (usually not *if*) our teenagers choose to lie to us.

Lying can be like a drug. It starts out innocently enough, just for fun. But at some point, a young person moves from telling lies to being "a liar." And when teenagers begin to define themselves in this way, they are setting time bombs that will eventually sabotage their future success.

Lying eats away at the fabric of a young person's character. It erodes his or her confidence. It creates a barrier to experiencing real intimacy, because it establishes a pattern of avoiding the challenges that come with facing the truth.

So you are wise to be concerned. But you don't actually have to "catch her in the act" of lying in order to provide your daughter feedback about her distrustful behavior. Try this: the next time she asks you to do something that you're just a little bit uncomfortable about, simply say (without any specific accusations and without any anxious emotion) that you simply "don't feel good about it" and that sometimes "a mom just needs to trust her gut."

When you give this answer, don't expect a thank-you note from your daughter; this answer will not likely calm her down. Instead it will likely make her more agitated. But you can actually let her frustration and annoyance work for you.

You see, up to this point, her lying has cost her very little in terms of freedom. She has been happy for you to "own the problem" of her lying. Up to this point, it seems obvious that you have been much more worried about her lying than she is.

When she asks why you "don't trust her," simply smile and let her know, "I would like to trust you without question, but this is one I just don't feel good about." She will want you to give reasons and examples, but don't take the bait. Put the ball back in her court by asking if she might have any ideas why you have had trouble trusting her absolutely. If she can't think of anything, invite her to get back with you when she thinks of something.

The message our kids need to hear loud and clear is that trust is easy to lose and hard to get back. She will do everything she can to make her distrustful behavior your problem. But by not giving her all the freedoms that she is normally used to, her distrustful behavior becomes her problem. Eventually, she may just hire you as a consultant to help her figure out how she can get the kind of freedom she really wants. When she does, you'll be tempted to tell her what to do (i.e., to make it your problem again). But instead, invite her to come up with a game plan for how trust might be rebuilt between the two of you.

While you are helping your daughter feel the frustrating consequences of her distrustful behavior, continue to find ways to catch her in the act of doing lots of things right. Provide encouragement and assurance that you are confident that she has what it takes to build the trust you are asking her to build. Find ways to praise progress, not perfection. And when she lies and then admits it quickly, don't be afraid to affirm her courage and growth.

There is nothing easy about this battle. But you will want to stand with your child on the side of her integrity, even when there are times when she will find your faithfulness horribly inconvenient.

Mark DeVries

54. This week our fifteen-year-old daughter lost her temper and said some very hurtful things to me. Then, fifteen minutes later, she acted like nothing happened and asked me to drive her to the mall. I couldn't believe it after what she had just said. Naturally I refused, and now things are pretty gloomy around our house. Is this kind of behavior normal?

Yes, your daughter's behavior is normal, but that doesn't make it right. Teenagers often use words defensively—as weapons—when they are with their peers and when they are with their parents and siblings. They lack the communication skills that come with age and experience. As the Bible teaches, "Reckless words pierce like a sword, / but the tongue of the wise brings healing" (Proverbs 12:18). Many teenagers (and sadly, many adults) haven't yet learned the wisdom of that proverb.

Use this occasion as a teachable moment. Talk to your daughter and let her know how you feel. Be specific about what she said and why you were hurt. Let her know that it especially hurts when someone you love speaks to you that way. Share how sometimes we can be completely oblivious to the disrespect and hurt in our words. We may blurt out names and accusations in anger that we really don't mean and later regret saying.

Your daughter may apologize, but she may not. Regardless, she will understand why you refused her request to take her to the mall. Hopefully she'll learn that her words have consequences. In this case, you will have to decide if any further discipline is required. If so, calmly explain the cause-and-effect relationship between your daughter's behavior and your response to it. Also explain that you trust that next time she is angry with you, she will think first and wait before speaking or yelling.

Remember, the emotions of an adolescent can turn on a dime. They can be angry one minute (doing or saying stupid things) and then a minute later act like nothing happened. Try not to take your daughter's outbursts personally or respond in anger yourself. Calmly help her to learn from her mistakes by connecting her behavior with consequences.

Dave Veerman

55. *Can you give me some ideas for consequences that work with teenagers? Most of the time when my fourteen-year-old messes up, I ground him. But if I keep that up he's going to be grounded for the rest of his life. Any other suggestions?*

Most teenagers have an "Achilles' heel"—a consequence that he or she would rather not face or a reward that works to motivate them toward good behavior. Sometimes they are difficult to identify, but they do exist.

Negative consequences work only when the consequence is bad

enough that your teenager wants to avoid it at all costs. You don't want them to choose the consequence over the good behavior because it's an easier pill to swallow. You also want consequences that you are going to be able to enforce and follow through on. Here are some of the most common negative consequences that have been known to work:

- *Loss of money.* Money is a big deal to teenagers (as it is to most people). You can discontinue his allowance/income, or your can create a schedule of "fines" for particular behaviors. If the fine can't be paid, then you can repossess some of his possessions and hold them until the fine is paid.

- *Loss of telephone.* Friends are very important to a teenager. Whether it's a cell phone or the phone in their room, restrictions on phone use can be very detrimental to the social life of a teen.

- *Loss of computer/instant messaging/e-mail privileges.* Kids love their computers and computer games, and they love being able to chat online with other kids. Taking this privilege away can be a great motivator.

- *Loss of freedom.* This is the "grounding" that you spoke of in your question. You can put all kinds of restrictions on where he can go or what he can do. Teenagers hate being treated like children, but if they can't behave responsibly like adults, you have no choice. A variation of grounding is a "reversal of restrictions." If you have loosened your restrictions (like curfew) as your teen got older, you can roll them back to earlier levels until the behavior is changed.

- *Loss of choice in clothes.* Taking away certain clothes can cause a crisis of major proportions for a teenager. This consequence would be appropriate only if the behavior is related to your teen's extreme choice of clothing.

- *Loss of car.* Any teen that is driving hates this one. By the way, keep in mind that it's very difficult to take something away from someone if it doesn't belong to you. That's why I recommend that you not give your teenagers their own car—or their own cell phone, computer, TV set, etc. Instead, "buy them for the family" but let them use them. That way, you retain control over them.

- *Loss of trust.* Earning and keeping your trust is very important to a teenager. For some teens, just knowing that their parents will no longer trust them can be a huge motivator. This will affect all future decisions that you make. ("Can we trust him?")

- *Loss of independence.* How will your teenager like it if you have to accompany him everywhere he goes? If you teenager has been ditching classes, then you go with him to class and (with the teacher's permission) sit next to him in class with your hair in rollers. That's sure to impress all his friends.

- *Loss of privacy.* Require him to keep the door to his bedroom wide open at all times, and inspect it daily, etc.

- *Loss of possessions.* Many teenagers have possessions that are very important to them (CD players, jewelry, cell phones, etc.). If your teenager understands that all his possessions can be "repossessed" as fines against their bad behavior, you can take them and hold them "in trust" until the behavior has been corrected.

- *Loss of time doing "good" things.* Sometimes kids need to know that their bad behavior affects all of life, not just the problem areas. Not being able to attend church youth group or play sports or spend time with the family—these are all things that are good and probably mean a lot to your teenager. These privileges can be lost as well.

Here are some other thoughts on consequences:

- Don't threaten a consequence that you can't carry out: "If you don't straighten up, you can find somewhere else to live." Likewise, don't overstate consequences: "You can't use the phone for the rest of the year!" That's fine if the rest of the year means two weeks. But if it means six months, you're in trouble.

- Once you make a rule, stick to it. Don't let your no become yes and your yes become no. Don't let your teen talk you out of your decisions once they are made. This undermines your authority.

- Be sure to monitor your teen's behavior. If you care about his behavior, then show you care by checking up on him. Sometimes parents come up with consequences and then (because they are afraid to ask) pretend they don't notice what's going on.

- Be unified as parents. When both parents are not in agreement on consequences, they are rarely effective.

- Be consistent. Don't have one consequence this time, another the next time and none the other times. It might be a good idea to write a contract or some other type of written agreement on behaviors and consequences so that your teenager will know what to expect. That will help him make good choices.

- The consequence should fit the offense. Try to make it both "related" and "reasonable." In other words, it's best when the consequence is somehow connected with the behavior. ("If you access pornography on the Internet, you will not be allowed to use the computer unsupervised.") Neither should the consequence be too harsh or too light.

Keep in mind that consequences are limited in what they can do. Some people would rather serve prison time than clean up their room. You'll have to learn what motivates your teenager and what doesn't. Sometimes the best motivator is not a consequence at all but a word of encouragement and affirmation from a parent who loves him very much.

Wayne Rice

56. *My son, who is almost seventeen, feels it's okay to go out at 11:30 to a friend's house to watch a movie, be home at 1:00 a.m. and be at work at 6:00 a.m. He's had trouble already with anxiety, and we feel he needs enough sleep before going in to work so early. How can we make him understand?*

At his age, your son probably needs to figure out for himself that you can't keep that kind of schedule and keep a job at the same time. He may discover (when he falls asleep on the job or loses his job) that he's only hurting himself. Teenagers learn best from experience, as you probably know.

Usually when you nag teenagers about things like this, it only makes them more determined to keep it up. When you let him decide for himself what to do, he may start making better decisions.

You can, however, exercise some parental authority and require him to choose between his job and a reasonable curfew. It all depends on which battles you believe are worth fighting.

Wayne Rice

> **DISCIPLINE AND DISCIPLINING**
>
> We most often think of discipline as punishment, a strict control to enforce obedience. But the root word of discipline is disciple. Disciples follow their teacher and learn all that they can in order to become like the teacher. In the same way, we can use the negative behaviors of our kids as opportunities to disciple them, to teach them.
>
> When discipline is mere punishment, the result is short term. If the only thing your kids learn from discipline is not to get caught next time, you haven't accomplished a whole lot. They need to learn the why of their actions so that they can learn from their experiences. When you use consequences and instruction together with a relationship based on love, your discipline will become discipleship.
>
> Jim Green

57. *Our fifteen-year-old daughter is so out of control that we've considered sending her to one of those camps in another state where they try to rehabilitate rebellious kids. We feel very ashamed to even discuss such a thing, but we don't know what else to do. We've tried all the "tough love" discipline that we know, but nothing seems to work. We really don't like the idea of sending her away, but what else can we do?*

First of all, don't be ashamed to consider anything that might save the life of your daughter. If she is as out of control as you believe she is, she may be in serious danger of harming herself or someone else. Tough love works both ways. It's not only tough on the teenager; it can be tough on parents. Parents who love their children will do whatever it takes to turn them around. If that means sending her away to a private boarding school, teen "boot camp" or some other residential rehabilitation facility, don't be afraid to do that.

But there may be other options. Don't give up on your daughter, and don't give up on yourself. Most behavioral problems take time to solve. Be patient and continue to provide loving yet firm discipline and consequences. Be strong and stay the course. Out-of-control teenagers are usually locked in a power struggle with their parents, and as long as they think they can win, they will continue trying to wear you down until you give up and give in. Don't let that happen. Hang in there, and remember that in most cases, things get worse before they get better. When parents stay the course, even the most rebellious teenagers can figure out that it's in their own best interest to change. Don't lose hope.

If you haven't done so already, get professional help. Seek counsel. Most parents who have out-of-control teenagers are too close to the situation and too emotionally involved to be objective. Even if your daughter is unwilling to go to a family counselor with you, an experienced counselor may be able to provide you with perspective, guidance and possible solutions that you have not considered before. Parenting was never meant to be done alone. There is strength in numbers. Parenting support groups, school counselors, youth workers and pastors are other sources of possible help, ideas and encouragement.

Sending your daughter to a boot camp or other facility may indeed be the best option for you and your daughter, but it should always be considered a last resort. Most teenagers don't go willingly, so there is almost always the traumatic experience of having the teenager "abducted" against her will. Most camps and schools are very expensive, costing thousands of dollars per month, and they usually require long-term stays of a year or more. Parental contact is usually not permitted for several months and then, when it is permitted, only for brief periods of time. I mention all this because the decision to send your daughter away should not be taken lightly. It will affect your daughter's life and your family's life in many ways, and there are no guarantees for success.

If you are seriously considering this option, do your homework. An Internet search for "teen boot camps" or "boarding schools" will get you started. There are literally hundreds of agencies and organizations that can help you locate the appropriate facility and program for your daughter. Likewise, there are many different kinds of camps and facilities, some Christian, some secular, some that focus on drug rehab, some that are like prisons, others that are more like private schools. Your "due diligence" is absolutely necessary. Make lots of phone calls, make personal visits, and get plenty of references for any facility that you are considering.

Do these programs work? Many programs do boast high success rates, but my personal experience has been that they rarely provide more than a temporary fix for deep-rooted behavioral problems.

When teenagers return to their former environment, they tend to fall back into the same patterns and behaviors as before. That's why it's usually best to find a solution at home, one that is permanent rather than temporary. What most teen boot camps and boarding schools provide is a highly structured environment with close supervision, clear rules, education in basic life skills and a strong support system that encourages good behavior. Perhaps you can find ways to provide those same things at home. You may need to make some huge changes in your life (you may need to move to another town or quit a job, for example), but sending your daughter away is a pretty big change too.

Just remember, your daughter is not a lost cause. She may be in danger, but she needs you now more than ever. Be that immovable object in her life that relentlessly loves and disciplines her. Take every opportunity you have to spend time with her, to work on your relationship. Watch for things she does right and encourage her. Brighten up the gloom with a positive attitude and a smile now and then. And of course, commit your daughter to the Lord in prayer every day. She belongs to him, not you, and he will help you get through this difficult time.

Wayne Rice

58. *My thirteen-year-old son has been diagnosed with ADHD. I really hate to keep him on Ritalin, but he can't concentrate or behave himself without it. Am I doing the right thing by making him take this medication?*

If your son has been diagnosed with ADHD (Attention Deficit Hyperactivity Disorder), then yes, you are doing the right thing by providing him with the medication he needs to function successfully in life. Most children who require medication for ADHD still need it as teen-

LIVING WITH ADHD: FIVE STEPS

1. *Do research.* If you suspect that your child has ADHD, read as many books on the subject as you can get your hands on. Here are a few suggestions to get you started:

   ■ Chris Zeigler Dendy, Teenagers with ADD: A Parents' Guide *(Woodbine House, 1995)*

   ■ David Stein, Ritalin Is Not the Answer *(Jossey-Bass, 1999)*

   ■ Dennis Swanberg, Diane Passno and Walt Larimore, Why A.D.H.D. Doesn't Mean Disaster *(Tyndale House, 2003)*

   There is also helpful information on the website of the National Institute of Mental Health <http://www.nimh.nih.gov>.

2. *Seek help.* Seek out professional help from someone who is properly trained and experienced with ADHD but doesn't see it as the only issue. To make an accurate diagnosis, a good clinician will do extensive testing, interviewing and evaluation of your child, taking into consideration every area of his or her life—psychological, social, emotional and intellectual factors as well as physical.

3. *Connect with others.* Create a network of mental health professionals, teachers, youth workers and other adults who will help provide support and accountability for your child. Request that they let you know when your child is acting out, especially when he or she is misbehaving or having other behavioral problems. Build a community of people around your child who care about his or her development.

4. *Provide love and support.* Many ADHD kids are able to function quite well, often without medication, when they have parents who are involved and generous with their love and support. By giving your child plenty of time, encouragement, discipline and understanding, you increase his or her chances for success in life.

5. *Find treatment.* If your doctor recommends medication, consider all of the alternatives. Ritalin is the most widely used, but there are others that are effective, including Concerta, Focalin and Adderall. Most are stimulants, but some are not. Children are not the same, nor are the medications. Whatever you try, monitor how the medication affects your child's behavior and watch for any side effects that may result. There may be headaches, nausea, intestinal problems or a racing heartbeat. In addition to medication, find out from your doctor or psychologist which behavioral strategies and therapies may be appropriate for your child.

David Olshine

agers and more than half of all adults with ADHD need it as well. If you have doubts regarding treatment (as you apparently do), then I would encourage you to seek advice from an experienced child psychiatrist or psychologist, pediatrician, or neurologist who can do a thorough assessment of your son's condition and make recommendations regarding the best therapy for your son. No single treatment is the answer for all children with ADHD.

What makes ADHD so troublesome (and controversial) is the diagnosis. According to the National Institute for Mental Health, the principal characteristics of ADHD are inattention (easily distracted), hyperactivity (constantly in motion) and impulsivity (acting before thinking). The problem is that most people would use those same characteristics to describe a normal thirteen-year-old. In fact, almost everyone exhibits those characteristics from time to time. Who hasn't blurted out something they didn't mean to say (impulsivity), jumped from one task to another (hyperactivity), or become disorganized and forgetful (inattention)?

The temptation for some parents and teachers is to use Ritalin (or other drugs) as a "quick fix" for controlling behavioral problems. Teachers can no longer discipline students as they did in the past with corporeal punishment or by enforcing strict consequences. Parents are often afraid of applying discipline or simply too exhausted to apply it when needed. Medications become a very tempting substitute for discipline, and unfortunately, there are doctors who are willing to prescribe them without a thorough and accurate diagnosis.

ADHD is a legitimate mental disorder, however, and it should not be left undiagnosed or untreated. Ordinarily it appears in children under the age of seven, handicapping them in most areas of life, including the classroom, the playground and the home. When ADHD children reach adolescence, problems continue and are often compounded by the normal challenges of being a teenager. Medication may be required to help your son succeed in life, but now more than ever you should do what every good parent needs to do—stay connected, keep the communication lines open, provide structure and clear limits along with a healthy dose of encouragement and love.

Wayne Rice

59. Our teenagers (two boys, fourteen and sixteen) have lately been using foul language a lot, and we've called them on it. But they insist we're old-fashioned and out of touch with reality. They say everybody talks that way and we should just get used to it. Are we wrong to set limits on their speech? When we were young, we would have had our mouths washed out with soap and water.

Maybe it's time to get out the soap and water again.

Just kidding.

For starters, don't be intimidated by what your sons think. You know what's right and wrong and that's all that matters as far as your household is concerned. Children don't make the rules, parents do.

Second, remember that attitudes formed at home will be carried with your kids into the outside world. There are standards and rules in the workplace, just as there are in the home. Bosses generally don't wash their employees' mouths with soap and water; they simply fire them. Profanity is rude and disrespectful to others. Unless your sons plan on working at a construction site or becoming bartenders, they should know that most businesses do not tolerate profanity. Polite and courteous behavior is necessary to be successful at school and work, in marriage and parenting. Better your sons learn this lesson at home rather than later on in life.

If you believe that profanity is wrong (and I hope you do), set your standards and stick to them. Make sure your kids know what kind of communication is allowed in your home and what is not: "In our home, we communicate with mutual respect. Profanity will not be tolerated from anyone, including parents. This includes cuss words of any kind, vulgarity or using God's name in vain." If you need to, make a list of words that are not allowed as well as the consequences for using them.

You can thank your sons for "enlightening" you about the "real world," but don't be afraid to enforce your rules. Obviously, there's a loss of respect here. In order to regain the respect of your sons, you must first learn to respect yourselves. Don't be a doormat. Don't beg for respect, yell or get angry. Respect comes from quiet strength that is calm and consistent.

Jim Green

DRUGS AND ALCOHOL

60. *We keep hearing all those terrible statistics about teenagers and drug use. We are so worried that our kids will start using drugs. What can we do to prevent that from happening?*

The first and best thing you can do is model good personal decisions about drug and alcohol use. Are you behaving the way you would like your teenagers to behave? Are you modeling responsible behavior? Remember that if you turn to drugs (even prescription drugs) or alcohol every time you feel bad, you're sending a message you probably don't want to send.

How about the friends your teens have chosen? Are they choosing to spend time with other teens who are making poor choices about drugs? Because that behavior is potentially very harmful and also illegal, you will have to step in as a parent to protect your teenager. By encouraging your teenagers to establish friendships with other teens who are making good choices about drugs and alcohol, you are encouraging your own children to make good choices.

Investing time in your teenagers is also a good way to prevent drug use. Being present at their events can encourage and support them. Eating meals together is another great time investment. When your teenagers know you are interested in them as individuals, they are less likely to damage your relationship through the use of drugs.

Be sure that your teenagers are in a good youth program, one that reinforces the standards you want your teens to follow. Also, give your teenagers resources that will educate them to the hazards of drug use. When used as a third source, a resource such as a health periodical or a newspaper article can become an educator as well. You and your teenagers can dialogue about the article, and the source becomes the teacher (the bad guy perhaps) and not you. Then you are not lecturing about the ills of drug use; you are merely providing information to your teen.

Kendra Smiley

61. *Our thirteen-year-old daughter has been caught drinking twice in the last four months. Apparently she drinks when she's with a certain group of friends. Should we be overly concerned about this?*

Overly concerned? You can't really be too concerned about this. Alcohol is a drug, and it is very dangerous. You should take steps right away to enforce a zero-tolerance rule on alcohol use for your daughter. Enforce it with consequences that will serve as an effective deterrent. Make sure you and your daughter know in advance what you will do if your daughter breaks the rules, and then follow through on it. If you need to do random breathalyzer tests on your daughter to get the truth, do it.

Your daughter may need an evaluation by a doctor or counselor. There may be physical or emotional problems that need to be addressed immediately. And if you drink yourself, give it up—at least until she's out of the house. While drinking in moderation may not be a problem for you, it may be for your daughter if she is looking to you as an example.

If you believe that her drinking is due to the friends she is keeping, then don't be afraid to put some limits on her relationships as well. It's not unreasonable for any parent to have this rule: "You will not, under any circumstances, spend time with kids who use drugs or alcohol, or who are engaged in any kind of illegal activity. Period." Again, you make the rule and enforce it. Zero tolerance.

Remember, your daughter is looking to you for some leadership here. She won't admit this, but most kids appreciate (if not now, they will later) their parents being strict and helping them to make a stand for what is right. It's hard for kids to resist peer pressure. It's much easier to say "My parents won't let me" or "I'll be in serious trouble if I do that" than to say no to bad behavior. Don't argue, just stick to your guns and take this issue very seriously. Your daughter is in very real danger.

Wayne Rice

LET'S TALK ABOUT ALCOHOL

It's important for parents to talk with their teens about alcohol. Here are some important points for you to communicate:

- *Adolescence is the absolute worst time anyone could ever drink alcohol. A teen's brain is growing rapidly, and alcohol kills off brain cells. Drinking damages the brain's ability to grow properly and could have a serious impact on a teen's mental health.*
- *When they drink with other kids, they are setting themselves up for big trouble. On dates, girls under the influence of alcohol become more pliant and boys become more aggressive. Alcohol is behind many a date-rape story. It's also behind hundreds of tragic stories of teens killed in auto accidents. (Check out M.A.D.D. for examples galore.)*
- *Most alcoholics begin drinking at an early age. People who stay away from alcohol during their teen years stand a better chance of becoming responsible drinkers in adulthood. There is a genetic disposition toward alcohol that runs in families. If your family has a history of alcoholism, there is an increased chance that your children will have a serious problem with alcohol in the future.*
- *Drinking is illegal before the age of eighteen in most states. When teens drink, they are breaking the law. They could be picked up by the police for drinking, and it will become part of their permanent record. Anyone who provides it for them is also at risk.*

Wayne Rice

62. My husband and I were becoming very suspicious of the way our fifteen-year-old son was acting. He had become increasingly rebellious and was hanging out with some kids who had been in trouble before. His grades were slipping and he repeatedly violated curfew. No amount of talking to him about these things did any good. My husband decided to search his room, and when he did, he found two pipes and evidence of marijuana. After first denying that it was his, our son finally admitted that he had smoked marijuana just once. He said he wouldn't smoke it again, but we aren't so sure. We think he has a problem and believe it's time to get some help. We are also considering moving him to a private school, away from his friends. He has threatened to run away if we make him change schools or lose his friends. We think this requires some serious discipline, but we don't want to drive him away from us either. We don't want to do more harm than good. What should we do?

First of all, your son does indeed have a problem. Remember that teenagers usually only admit to what they think you already know. You caught him with some drug paraphernalia so he is forced to admit to at least using the stuff once. You can be certain that he has used it more than once, but that's irrelevant. You have all the evidence you need to take action now. The price of inaction is unacceptably high.

Unfortunately, whenever you try to turn a situation like this around, you can expect things to go from bad to worse before they get better. Your fears about losing your son are justified. When you exercise your parental authority and place limits on what he can do, he may rebel even more. He'll probably fight you and do everything he can to cause you to change your mind or simply give up. It won't be easy, and you won't see immediate results. But you have to do it anyway.

The first place to start is probably with an evaluation by a doctor or drug counselor. You need to know the extent of your son's problem. Perhaps some drug education is in order—not so much for him, but for you. The more you know, the better your decisions will be. That's not always the case with teenagers. Most kids have all the information they need. They just don't have the experience and the strength of character to make good choices. Luckily for him, you can provide the experience he needs and a few character-building activities that will help him make better choices in the future. That's where discipline comes in.

What kind of discipline should be implemented? That depends a lot on your son, his personality, his history and other factors too numerous to list here. But one good place to start is with his friends. Since he has proven that he is not capable of making good choices about who he hangs out with, you can start by making that choice for him. New rule: from this day forward, he is forbidden, absolutely and completely, to have any contact with any of the kids in his former group of friends. This is not for just a few days, weeks or months. This is forever. His relationship with those particular kids (identify them by name) is officially over—end of discussion. Sound harsh? Absolutely—but you know and he knows that without those friends, there would have been no drug use. Friends like those are no friends at all, and there's no point in trying to save them for later. He can remain in the same school, the same town, and enjoy the same privileges he always had—so long as he doesn't violate this rule. You will have to monitor this closely, of course.

On the positive side, tell him that you're going to help as much as you can by spending a lot of time together as a family and helping him find other things to do. You can encourage him to get involved in a church youth group or some other positive peer-group experience. Obviously you can't force friends on him or make him do anything that he doesn't want to do, but he needs to understand that he's being given a second chance to make better choices about his friends and activities. There won't be a third chance. In other words, if you ever find out that he's spending time with any of his old friends again or participating in any drug-related activities, he'll be under house arrest for the entire summer and transferred to a new school in the fall. Other consequences can be implemented as well, such as random drug tests, loss of privileges and the like.

Remember, this kind of discipline is not easy. Things will get worse before they get better. But the "worse" that you create by being a good parent will be a lot easier for you to handle than the "worse" that will happen if you don't. Not easy, but easier. Stand firm and let your son know by your actions that you love him enough to do whatever it takes to turn his life around.

Wayne Rice

63. We let our two teenagers drink alcoholic beverages (wine, some cocktails) at home with us, but we don't allow them to drink when they are with their friends or away from home. We believe that we are teaching our children to drink responsibly. What do you think?

First, how do you know they're not drinking away from home? Second, isn't it against the law for minors (under eighteen or twenty-one) to drink alcohol in your state?

I appreciate the fact that you desire to teach your children to drink responsibly because there is so much abuse of alcohol. But not everything has to be learned from experience. You wouldn't want your kids to learn about drug abuse by doing drugs, or the dangers of sexual abuse by having sex. Maybe you could teach them how to drink responsibly by acting responsibly yourself and not allowing them to drink at this early age. Alcohol is an acquired taste. Maybe it's one best left till later in life.

Drinking is the number one destructive drug of our culture. It is at the center of heartache and pain in abusive family relationships, with wives and children the most common victims. A very high percentage of crimes are committed under the influence of alcohol. Most drug addicts will tell you they started with alcohol before moving on to their drugs of choice. Alcohol is also the number one cause of fatal automobile accidents. The list goes on. Talk to your kids about the dangers of alcohol and drug abuse.

Children learn life skills and behaviors from watching their parents. They will most often duplicate how we drive, how we treat people, how we live out our faith and values, and how we drink.

You asked for an opinion. I would not allow my teenager to drink alcohol at home. You can teach responsibility by being a good example for them and teaching them to live by the rules that are in place.

Jim Green

64. I smoked pot and did drugs when I was a kid. Now I'm afraid my teenager is going to ask me whether I did or not. Should I tell him the truth or lie about it?

Well, we can't recommend lying, but we can definitely recommend that you avoid giving your teenager the rope he may end up hanging *you* with. As a general rule, you should never volunteer self-incriminating information to anyone unless the information is absolutely essential to the point you are about to make. Of course, when it comes to the issue of drugs, it's hard to imagine what the point might be.

Here are a few things to consider before you tell all:

■ *The age of the teenager.* It's probably not necessary for any teenager under the age of seventeen or eighteen to know just how dumb you were as a kid. Rather than learning anything useful, he'll only feel a sense of loss and disappointment, maybe shock. Most kids prefer to hang on to their childhood images of mom and dad as strong, heroic figures for as long as possible.

- *The maturity of the teenager.* Let's face it, some kids simply don't know how to process information very well. Rather than getting the message "Gosh, my parents know what they're talking about. Maybe I should listen to them," they instead get "Dude! My parents used drugs and they turned out okay. So what's the big deal?"

- *The motive of the teenager.* Why does your teenager want to know? If he is involved in drug use or engaged in an argument with you about the subject, there's a strong likelihood he is only looking for a way to justify his own bad behavior. Don't give him ammunition he can, and likely will, use against you now or later.

Simply put, you are under no obligation whatsoever to confess your sins to your teenager. There are some things that are best left unsaid. Plead the fifth if you must. You might just remind him that what you did as a teenager is totally irrelevant: "So what if I did drugs? Let's pretend for a minute that I did. What does that have to do with making right decisions?" The answer, of course, is nothing at all, so that gives you permission to move on to another subject.

You can also answer by focusing instead on what you did right. "When I was a teenager, I saw firsthand how drugs could mess up your life. That's when I made the decision to never use them." Leave it at that.

On the other hand, if your teenager is old enough and mature enough and has given you no reason to worry about drug use, then answering the question forthrightly is probably not going to be a problem. Many parents do enjoy a mutually open, honest and trusting relationship with their kids. Like many issues, this is a judgment call that requires real sensitivity to the risks of revealing too much information.

Wayne Rice

8

APPEARANCE

65. *Our fourteen-year-old daughter is quite well developed for her age, and she insists on wearing tight, revealing clothes and excessive makeup. Naturally she is starting to attract older boys, and this worries us . . . a lot. We've asked her to dress more modestly, but she just gets angry and insists that she has the right to choose her own clothes. Is it wrong for us to set limits on what she can wear?*

It isn't wrong for you to limit what your daughter can wear. In fact, it's your right and your responsibility. Your goal, however, should be to work together on this. Most girls don't have a clue what goes on in a guy's mind when he sees a girl dressed provocatively, especially a young woman as attractive as she is. Without implying that all guys have dirty minds, let her know what boys are like, what they think (or will think) and how they talk. How does she want others (especially boys) to think of her? What would she think if her mother dressed that way? And how would she feel if she saw men leering at her mom and making suggestive comments about her?

Explain to her that you understand a lot of kids her age are dressing that way and that the latest styles can be pretty revealing. The goal is to dress modestly and in style. Tell her that it won't be easy, but it is possible, and you are willing to help. At this point, you may want to suggest a shopping trip to buy some attractive but not overly revealing outfits. This will cost you time and money, but it will be worth the investment.

Dave Veerman

66. Our fourteen-year-old son is probably the shortest boy in his entire freshman class. He has always been small for his age, but it seems that he's a late bloomer, too. We've assured him that he'll probably get bigger, but meanwhile, some of the other boys call him names (midget, dwarf, etc.) and tease him unmercifully. Should we come to his rescue? We really feel bad for him.

Let your son know that you know it's tough and that you feel for him. Don't minimize the pain or gloss over his feelings; they're real, and kids at school can be very unkind. If you (or your spouse) were a late bloomer, share some of your experiences so he knows you share his pain. But also let him know when you had your growth spurt. Find other men who grew late, and use them as examples as well.

Rather than rescuing your son from the teasing and name calling, give him other opportunities to succeed: music, drama, hobbies and other activities. In many sports, being small is not a liability; in fact, in some (wrestling, gymnastics, diving, etc.) it can be an asset. If your son loves basketball but has been cut from the team for being small (and you are 6'6" and know he will probably grow to your height), remind him that even Michael Jordan was cut from a high school basketball team (true). Then encourage him to continue to develop his skills so he'll be ready when the growth comes. In all of this, however, be sure to keep affirming him as a valued creation of God and your special son.

Dave Veerman

67. *I want my teenager to look presentable when he attends church and other family functions, but he refuses. How can we settle this without fighting and arguing?*

Here's a start: stop fighting and arguing. As long as your focus is on the relative merits of dressing up or not dressing up for certain functions, this argument will never end. Remember the "save your breath" principle. If you realize that there is nothing you can say to change your son's opinion, save your breath. The more you talk about it, the more the two of you become polarized and the more he will begin to link his core identity to not dressing up. This is not a battle you can win with words.

Realistically, what your son wears or doesn't wear is really "background noise" to the larger issue here—respect. If he doesn't learn the value of showing respect for authority before he moves into adulthood, he will be set up for a life of frustrating defeats at work, in relationships and with the law. Respect is definitely one worth going to the mat over.

But you don't need to argue about it. Though there is likely

PULL UP YOUR PANTS

At one of our *Understanding Your Teenager* seminars, a dad shared with me this incident with his son.

One Sunday morning as the family was leaving for church, the dad asked his teen son to pull up his pants. He was wearing them very low, with his underwear showing and his pant legs dragging on the ground.

"But dad," the son insisted, "this is how everybody wears their pants!" Grudgingly, he pulled up his pants, but they didn't stay there very long.

This scenario repeated itself several weeks in a row. Finally the dad came up with an idea. He bought himself a pair of baggy pants and some colorful boxer shorts. The next Sunday morning as the family was leaving for church, he wore them very low with his underwear showing. When his son saw his dad dressed that way, he was in shock. "DAD! What do you think you're doing? You can't wear your pants like that!"

The dad made a deal with his son. If he promised to wear his pants where they belonged, so would he.

The problem was solved.

Wayne Rice

little you can do to change your son's opinion, there is actually a good deal you can do to change his behavior. Simply set up clear and immediate consequences for any disrespectful behavior (including refusing to wear clothes that you consider appropriate). With a respectful smile, say something like this: "Son, I realize that I have been spending way too much time worrying about what you wear to church and other functions, and I am no longer going to try to talk you into doing those things. I've realized that the way you dress is not the issue at all. Respect is. And when you choose to dress in a way that seems disrespectful to me, I will let you know. Then the choice is up to you. If you choose to dress respectfully, you will enjoy all the freedoms you have been used to. If you choose to dress disrespectfully, the car (or the computer or the phone or the TV or the Xbox or the weekend freedom or the allowance, etc.) will not be available to you until your next opportunity to dress respectfully."

Your son, if he has a pulse, will respond by saying that he doesn't think his clothes are disrespectful. If he is really good, he may even argue that you are "imposing your values on him." (At this point, celebrate that your son is using good formal operational thinking, learning to sharpen his brain by trying to argue with you.)

"Right," you can say. "I am imposing the value of respect on you. Your whole life you will be surrounded by people in authority who may not be as smart as you are but who you still need to respect. Whether it's a boss, a teacher or a policeman, you will need to learn to practice respect, even when you don't particularly agree with the person in authority. Today, I just happen to be the authority. You can choose to respect me or not, but—just like in real life—disrespect will not get you the kind of freedom you want."

Once you've made your speech and made your consequences clear (one time only!), put your plan into action.

When (not if) your son is disrespectfully dressed, let him know *once* that he is dressed disrespectfully (in four words or less). Don't ask him to change clothes. Don't tell him there will be a consequence. Don't nag or yell. When it's time to leave for the event, smile and say, "Okay, let's go." Don't mention his clothes again until you get home. When you get home, remind him that he made a choice not to have access to the car (or the computer or the phone, etc.) until his next opportunity to dress respectfully.

You will know that the consequence is appropriate because he will become anxious and frustrated ("That's not fair!" "You didn't warn me!" etc.). At this point, don't step into the argument. You can't teach respect by being disrespectful yourself, in spite of the energetic and argumentative ways that he may choose to respond. Simply smile and say, "I'm sorry you made the choice you did, but the consequence will stand until you dress respectfully for another event."

Here's a fascinating fact: the more calm you are, the more anxious he will be. And the more anxious he is, the more likely it is that he will make a decision to change his behavior. However, this doesn't sound like a fight he will be willing to give up easily, so don't step onto the playing field unless you are ready to take a few hits.

Mark DeVries

68. *I know we should pick our battles wisely, but our teenager wants a tattoo. Over my dead body! I know this is not a huge moral issue, but I absolutely am not going to allow my kid to ruin his appearance with a stupid tattoo which is permanent. Needless to say, we're fighting over this one, but I wonder . . . is it worth all the hassle?*

First, don't let anyone else (including me) dictate what is the right thing to do for your family. You have every right to make and enforce whatever rules you believe are important for your family. It's obvious from your question that you do care about the long-term welfare of your teenager. You, like most of us who are older, know that there will come a day when he will regret many of the decisions made during the teen years. That tattoo will be a constant reminder of one bad decision in particular.

Next time you find yourself getting drawn into an argument with your teenager over this issue, just walk away. Save your breath. Just make your rules and enforce them. Don't expect your teenager to say, "Gosh, Dad, I never thought of that before. Thanks for sharing that helpful information with me. You're absolutely right. I sure don't want to be stupid like all my friends." I don't think any teenager has said that in the history of the world.

However, as a general rule of thumb, we do recommend that as your teenagers get older you learn to save your energy for issues with serious moral consequences. That doesn't mean you have to like what your teenager does. It just means you don't let it destroy the relationship that you have with your teen. Sometimes it's best to let them make their own decisions and live with the consequences if they aren't seriously harmful.

It might be helpful to try and see things from your teen's perspective. Everybody he knows seems to be getting a tattoo. It's a form of personal expression these days. Even though we think tattoos look terrible, the kids think they look cool. And when we say, "Someday you'll regret it!" we need to remember that many in his generation will experience the same regret. Chances are pretty good that his boss, or his employees, will all have tattoos as well. It will be *their* kids who think they look dumb.

To show yourself as empathetic a dad as possible, you might offer your teenager this window of opportunity: "When you are eighteen, if you still want a tattoo, be my guest. Cover yourself with tattoos and join the circus." In some states, you have to be eighteen to get a tattoo anyway. Regardless, you can't control what they do forever.

However, if you do decide to allow a tattoo before the age of eighteen, consider allowing it only if it passes inspection by mom and dad. You have to approve the design: what it says, where it goes and who does it. And of course, they must pay for it themselves. If these rules are disobeyed, you will personally escort them to a tattoo artist to have it removed—again at their own expense.

Here are some issues that you can discuss with your teenager regarding tattoos:

- Why do you want it? Everyone else having one is not a very good reason to get one yourself. Tattoos usually symbolize one's values, beliefs, lifestyle choices, identity, important relationships, milestones in life and so on. It's important to think this through carefully since it's a lifetime commitment.

- What are the health risks? Tattooing is an invasive procedure, like having your blood drawn or getting a shot. Any time a needle is inserted into your skin, you run the risk of getting an infection or contracting a dangerous virus like hepatitis B, or even AIDS.

- What is your pain threshold? While most people can handle it, not everyone can.

- What kind of design do you want, and who will design it?

- What if you change your mind? What is involved in having a tattoo removed? While it is possible to remove tattoos with laser skin treatment, it is expensive and not covered by health insurance. It's also painful and leaves scars in most cases.

Your teenager may say to you, "But it's *my* body!" Well, actually, it's not. His body belongs to God. We are asked to present our bodies as "living sacrifices, holy and pleasing to God" (Romans 12:1). The Bible also teaches, "Do you not know that your body is a temple of the Holy Spirit? . . . You are not your own" (1 Corinthians 6:19). These verses don't necessarily mean tattoos are forbidden, but they should certainly make us think twice before we put graffiti on the temple of God.

Wayne Rice

69. Our fourteen-year-old daughter wants to get her navel pierced, but we don't think this is appropriate for girls her age, or any age for that matter. What should we do?

Your daughter is likely very aware of the current fashion of exposed midriffs, tight abs and belly-button piercing. Piercings are more of a gray area than tattoos because they aren't permanent. If she got her belly-button ring now and then decided when she was sixteen that it was no longer fashionable, she could simply take it out and the hole would fill in.

The deeper issue in this situation is teaching her to think beyond the "here and now" urgency that is driving her desire to get the piercing. Does she want to get this because other fourteen-year-olds have them? Will she be asking for a tattoo next? You will probably have to get below the surface and find out what is driving this. If it's primarily a fashion statement, I'd be more likely to let her get her navel pierced on her fifteenth birthday; but if it's because "I have to fit in," I'd be less likely to give in.

Let me explain. Sometimes teens want to do things that annoy us as adult parent-types. We did the same thing when we were teens. It's about "individuation"—the process of becoming independent from parents. A certain amount of this is necessary for adolescents. It's not easy for the teen or the parent, but it is a part of growing up. We need to think of ways that allow our teens to be different from us (and at times weird), but hopefully not in a damaging or permanent way.

But you also want to guard your teen from giving in to the latest form of peer pressure. You want her to be able to stand alone, so that when temptations come her way, she can say, "No thanks, I'll pass." In this case, your job is to discern if it's an issue of individuation or an act of compliance to peer pressure. Let her know that you want her to be able to express herself but that you don't want her to fall victim to peer pressure—even if it's something as harmless as a belly-button ring.

Tim Smith

9

ENTERTAINMENT

70. *When I was a teenager, we listened to rock and roll, but it wasn't nearly as filthy and vulgar as the music is today. How worried should I be about the music our kids are listening to?*

You're right—the times and the music have changed. And there's no doubt that popular music today can be "filthy and vulgar." Be careful criticizing your teenager's music, however, because it probably will be interpreted as a criticism of your teenager's friends. Many kids don't like the music when they first begin listening to it. But their friends seem to, and it's the soundtrack of their culture. So music becomes a way for them to show that they belong and are growing up.

You ask if you should be worried about the music. In a word, yes. Our kids shouldn't be filling their minds with garbage. On the other hand, prohibiting them from listening to it will probably drive them to it. This is a good opportunity to guide rather than block. At some point, preferably away from the house, have a good talk about a variety of entertainment options. And explain your concern for your teenager and the kind of person that he or she is becoming.

Further, explain that you aren't against the style of music or even the volume. What bothers you are the subtle and even very explicit messages of the songs and, being totally frank, the lifestyles of some of the performers. Then ask for your son or daughter's ideas about other radio stations, artists, etc., that aren't nearly so objectionable and may even present positive messages and role models. This might be a good time for a field trip to a music store so your teenager can find the popular CDs and you can listen and read the lyrics together.

Dave Veerman

71. *What can we do to put restrictions on our teenager's choices of music and entertainment? Are there any rules that we can put in place to limit his exposure to harmful influences?*

Well, obviously age is a factor here. But let's assume you have a fifteen-year-old son and his favorite band is some guys who call themselves Rancid Puss, and although you can't understand their lyrics, you have a gut feeling that their stuff is somewhere to the far side of "I Want to Hold Your Hand." You don't like the values they represent, and frankly, the guy with the spike in his lower lip is hard for you to look at.

First of all, I would really encourage you to listen to the CD with your teenager. Ask him what it is he likes about the music. You might find out something about the band that you didn't know. Even better than that, you might find out something about your son that you didn't know. And here's another cool thing: he might find out something about you that he didn't expect.

Second, make sure that your concerns about his music are over substance and not style. If it's just a matter of volume, tempo, instrumentation or spike placement, you may be wiser to simply let it go. Your son doesn't insist that you act like a teenager and enjoy his music and art. Make sure you're not requiring him to act like an adult and enjoy your music or art.

Third, remember that the goal is to teach discernment. This is sort of the inverse of the old adage "Give a man fish and he can eat for a day; teach him to fish and he can eat for a lifetime." In this case, it's get rid of the poison today and your son has one less toxic CD; teach him to identify poison and he can stay detoxed for a lifetime. Just telling him to flush his music down the toilet is bad both for the plumbing and for long-term learning. If you have problems with a song or a band, talk them over with him so that he can understand your concerns. This will work toward your goal of shaping his capacity for discernment.

Along these lines, you might encourage your son to make his own CD or digital music collection by showing discernment in the songs he copies or downloads for his own enjoyment. If he has a digital music player (like Apple's iPod or Dell's Digital Jukebox), he can be much more selective about the music he chooses to listen to.

Finally, don't win the battle at the expense of losing the war. You can win the battle over whether the music will be in the house. In some ways, that's easy. But ultimately, the bigger battlefield is not your son's ear but his heart. And that battle is not so easily won. Recent world events have reminded us that sometimes it's easier to win the war than to win the peace. Age and attitude are crucial factors here. However, this might be an area where compromise is a better strategy than victory. This battle may not end with you being thrilled with all of the music that your son listens to. But perhaps the greater victory is that the conflict ends with your son feeling that, even though he may have to alter some of his listening habits, he has been heard.

Duffy Robbins

72. *We don't allow our teenager to go see (or rent) R-rated movies, but what if he watches R-rated movies at a friend's house? We can't control what other people allow their kids to do.*

You are right to say that you can't control what other people allow their kids to do. In fact, you can't really control what your son or daughter does outside your home, especially in high school. Let's face it, the older they become, the more independent they get. And that's not bad—we want our kids to grow up and become responsible adults. That's the point here, and it provides a good opportunity in this stage of parenting.

At an appropriate time, share your concerns about certain movies, videos, TV shows and other entertainment options. Explain the GIGO principle (garbage in, garbage out) and talk about Romans 12:2 and Philippians 4:8, which teach us to guard our minds. It's not easy to erase pornographic and violent images, and negative thoughts can lead to negative actions. What we see does affect how we act (if that wasn't true, why would advertisers spend so much money on their images?). And the values presented can be even more destructive than the visual images. Give examples to help your kids become discerning in this area.

Be sure to acknowledge that you can't control everything they do, and soon you won't be able to control anything—but that's okay because you want them to grow into responsible adults with character and integrity. Encourage them to build their own convictions and to stand on them, regardless of what anyone else says or does. You might suggest to your teen that he respectfully excuse himself from watching objectionable movies when he is at friends' homes. This demonstrates maturity and strength of character.

Finally, explain trust. Let your teenager know that you want to trust him. In fact, you do trust him to make the right decisions and to tell you the truth. Remind him, however, that when trust is broken, it's not easily repaired. If he is unwilling or unable to make good decisions about his entertainment choices, then you will have to set limits for him until he can.

Dave Veerman

73. *Should we allow our fourteen-year-old to have a TV in his room? We've been thinking that this would solve the conflicts we often have regarding what shows to watch. What do you think?*

No. (How's that for a quick answer?) Here's why.

First, most families already watch too much TV. Instead of interacting, talking, and having fun and adventure together, they sit and watch others interacting, talking, and having fun and adventure. One more television, especially one that isolates your fourteen-year-old from the rest of the family, will only make the situation worse.

Second, the "in his room" part of the deal can be a problem. Besides isolating him from the family, the TV set can be a powerful distraction from doing homework. Instead, work out a deal in which your son can watch certain TV programs after finishing his schoolwork, chores or whatever else he needs to do.

Third, most kids consider everything in their rooms to be "theirs," as in "It's my TV!" That's okay, except when followed by the implicit or explicit philosophy, "So I can watch whatever I want," leading to a different argument. Having more than one television is fine (and may help resolve the issue of what shows to watch), but all the sets should be seen as belonging to the family, under the supervision of mom and dad.

You raise an important issue—how to resolve the conflict regarding what shows to watch. Certainly you should have guidelines that relate to television viewing by all members of the family. But (I know this is a stretch, but bear with me) occasionally more than one high quality and desirable program may be broadcast at the same time (for example, ESPN for dad, HGTV for mom and a sitcom for junior). So even in the case of multiple sets, conflicts may occur. This is where you, as the mature adult, get to model compromise. That is, don't always insist on watching your program—give others the opportunity to watch their favorites too. You might consider buying TiVo or some brand of digital recorder so that you can watch the quality programs when you want to watch them. You get to be the programmer for TV and skip the commercials. You can schedule shows that the whole family enjoys together and make it an event, at a time that is convenient for everyone.

Some families limit TV watching to a set number of hours a week per family member. In other words, each person is allowed to choose a determined number of programs. But each person must limit the amount of time that he or she spends in front of the tube to a set amount of hours per week (no carryover). The numbers for both categories don't have to be the same for every family member (just as bedtimes and so forth vary depending on age and other factors), but every family member, including parents, should submit to the system. This will lead to healthy discussion and decision making, and perhaps even to conversation and alternative family entertainment.

Dave Veerman

10

TECHNOLOGY

74. We bought our teenager a computer, and now he spends six to eight hours a day sitting in front of it. He's either playing video games or online chatting with friends. I worry that he's not getting enough exercise or learning any other skills. He just sits there staring at that screen for days. When I try to set some limits on how much time he uses the computer, he thinks I'm being unfair and paranoid. Besides, it's his computer, he says, and he knows what he's doing. Should I be worried, or is this normal?

You are absolutely right to be concerned about that kind of computer use. The physical, social and emotional issues you raise are very real and shouldn't be ignored. I hate to be too blunt about this but I need to ask, "Who's in charge here?" You are the parent. You bought the computer and I assume you're paying for the connection, so it's quite appropriate for you to set limits on how it can be used. Obviously that will be tougher now that certain patterns have been established, but the longer you wait, the harder it will be to turn things around. I'm sure if you had it all to do over again you would have laid out the rules from the beginning.

Let's be balanced on this. A lot of video games are good fun and can be a wonderful way for a kid to relax and relieve a bit of stress, and we better get used to the fact that online communication is the way kids today stay connected with each other. Unfortunately, this is another good thing that can turn ugly with abuse. Not only can a computer become addictive, it also represents a gateway to lots of stuff that you should be legitimately afraid about. I probably don't need to remind you of the inappropriateness of lots of games that are on the market (or available online), and I'm sure you're aware of the amount of dangerous material that lurks on the Web just a click or two away from your home.

I assume you've got some kind of a filter on your Internet connection that will provide a measure of safety for your son. Some families have chosen to put their computer in a high traffic area of their home to raise the level of accountability (for both their kids and themselves) and make it easier to monitor the time kids spend on it. There's even a gadget available that lets you load a weekly time limit onto a "credit card" and makes kids swipe the card to get online. When they've used up their time they're done until the card is renewed.

Computers have the power to create a fantasy world that plenty of people escape to. It might be worth asking whether that might be the case for your son. Are there things going on in his world that make the world of video games an attractive alternative? Is there an issue in your home or family that makes it safer to live in cyberspace than in the real world?

Sit down with your son and do an evaluation now that the computer has been in the house for a while. Decide together what the boundaries will be and then commit to firmly enforcing them.

Marv Penner

75. Should we provide our teenager with her own cell phone? We are

afraid that she will lose it or run up the phone bill. And we aren't sure it's a good idea for her to be on the phone talking to friends all the time.

Isn't technology great? Just a few years ago, parents would give their teenagers a quarter and the instructions, "Use this to call me when . . ." Now, with the proliferation of cell phones, kids have no excuse not to call.

Besides keeping in touch, cell phones can be used to get assistance or directions when the car breaks down or a person is lost. And with some of the calling plans the cell phone can provide an inexpensive alternative to the traditional long-distance telephone bills.

You raise a good point, however—a teenager may lose the phone, run up the bill or talk to friends all the time. But don't think of this as an all-or-nothing decision. In other words, just as you would with driving and other privileges, you can use the question of cell phone usage as the opportunity to help your daughter handle responsibility. You can begin by providing a phone and then monitoring its use (a set amount of minutes per day, week, weekend or whatever). As she demonstrates responsible use of her phone, you can increase her freedom to use it. If, on the other hand, she is irresponsible with its use, be sure to enforce specific consequences (for example, requiring her to pay for the extra charges from her allowance, restricting phone use further, making her pay for the lost phone or taking the phone away for a time).

One final point: remember that teenage girls enjoy socializing via the phone. Depending on the calling plan, they could spend hours on the phone daily without incurring huge charges. Yet these calls can become convenient homework interrupters or delayers. So feel free to limit phone use during chores, schoolwork, church, family times and other important activities. Just because someone owns a phone doesn't mean he or she can and should use it anytime.

Dave Veerman

76. Our son has his own e-mail account on our family computer, but we have set it up so that we screen all his e-mails before he sees them. He's only fourteen years old. He has asked us not to screen his e-mail because it's a violation of his right to privacy. But we're afraid of the unsolicited e-mails (spam) that we really don't think he should see. How should we handle our son's request?

First—and I have to say this up front even though the reference comes in the middle of your question—your son's right to privacy doesn't mean he can do anything he wants. Nobody has that right. Second, until he is eighteen, you are responsible for him. He doesn't get the rights and privileges of adulthood until he is out of your house and on his own.

Unfortunately, today's parents become very intimidated when they are accused of violating their children's "rights" for fear that they are guilty of child abuse, illegal activity or (worse) not being as good as other parents (gasp). Relax and take a deep breath. You are the parent and you have the right *and* the responsibility to know what's going on in your home—period.

Okay, now back to the issue of computer use. It's permissible and even advisable to monitor computer use, just as you monitor television use. In fact, because of the predatory nature of pornographers and the strong temptation for adolescent boys to give in and check out pornographic images, the computers used by kids should be in a relatively public or open area of the house. It's not that parents will always be looking over their son or daughter's shoulders, but the prospect that they could or might happen to walk by will usually help the teen resist temptation. The same is true for chat rooms.

Don't be afraid to set limits for your teenager regarding computer use. If he wants to continue using the computer, then he needs to agree to automatically delete e-mails from people he doesn't know and *never* open attachments from an unknown source. Make sure he understands that the privilege of using the computer comes with great responsibility.

You probably don't have to screen your son's e-mails unless you are aware of a problem. On the other hand, you could screen them for a while and then back away as your son demonstrates maturity and good judgment in this area. If you want to avoid screening his e-mail yourself, consider installing the kind of software that will do it for you. There are many e-mail providers and Internet services that have ways to screen unwanted spam and objectionable content automatically. This is a good idea not only for teenagers but for parents as well.

Just as with any other technological tool, computers can be used for good or evil. We can find almost anything online (news, weather, directions, products, etc.). And what a tremendous resource for education and research! But the Internet has also been used by pedophiles, swindlers, hackers and worse. Encourage your son's computer literacy, but steer him away from becoming enslaved by it.

Dave Veerman

77. *Our daughter is online quite a bit, usually visiting chat rooms, having "conversations" with other people from all over the world. We worry quite a bit about this because of horror stories we've heard, but we don't want to overreact. Any suggestions?*

What's so striking to me is that this is an issue that didn't even exist when I started out in youth ministry thirty years ago. Back then, when we said "Log on!" we meant, "I'm cold!" Now, those words take us through a portal that can lead us to places of virtual community, unending curiosity and deep depravity. And none of us really knows how all of this nonstop access and accessibility is going to change our lives and our communities in the years to come.

That's why I suggest first and foremost that parents talk to their kids about this stuff. Make your concerns known. Don't underestimate the impact of your thoughts and feelings when your child is involved in behavior that causes you concern.

It's true, you don't want to overreact. If we're honest, we all understand that as parents who love our children we are prone to be overprotective: "Honey, she's in there on the Disney website again. We've got to do something! Don't you realize that Britney Spears started out as a Mouseketeer?" The Internet has much that is positive to offer our children.

On the other hand, when we are completely mum about our concerns, we communicate to our child that either (a) there is no danger here; or (b) I feel there is danger here, but you don't care about or respect my feelings so I won't share them; or (c) there is danger here, but I don't want to go to the trouble of warning you about it.

When you do speak to your daughter about your concerns, be sure to do it in a way that is informative without being enticing. I remember as a teenager hearing testimonies about all the bad stuff that could happen if I were to pursue certain sins, and the testimonies were so lurid and vivid that we couldn't wait to put ourselves in harm's way. What you don't want is a child who is surfing around on the net to see what all the fuss is about.

Second, and this may offend your sense of interior decoration, I strongly recommend putting the computer where there is a lot of foot traffic. Part of the computer's seduction is that it offers us anonymity. It allows us to venture to places we might not normally go without the accountability that we might normally expect. A computer in a teenager's room offers much greater risk than a computer in the den or in a corner of the kitchen.

Third, and this suggestion is related to the previous one, get the biggest, baddest monitor you can find—a screen so large that its images are clearly visible from across the room. Forty years ago, parents fretted about a teenage daughter camouflaging her racy romance novel behind a Jane Austen book, or about a teenage son who hid his girlie magazine under the bed. But all of that would have been much more difficult to do if the novel had been printed on a seventeen-inch screen, or if the magazine were "hidden" in plain view in the family room. Part of fighting temptation is eliminating the battlefields, or at least keeping the enemy from going underground.

Finally, maybe it's because I grew up in the Cold War years, but when it comes to the Internet and cable TV, I endorse a policy of "trust but verify." Take advantage of the various blocking software that is available. If your concerns have grown into suspicions, you might even inquire about tracking software that keeps digital records of websites visited. Ultimately you have to want to trust your daughter in these matters. But every day sad stories remind us that there are very untrustworthy people on the Internet—virtual spiders—who stalk and prowl the World Wide Web. You are wise to be on your guard.

Duffy Robbins

11

SCHOOL

78. *Our fifteen-year-old hates school. We aren't sure what the problem is, but he refuses to study or do his homework. Sometimes he fakes being sick so he can stay home. We know that our son is smart enough to pass his classes, but he just lacks motivation. Do you have any suggestions on how to motivate teenagers to take school seriously?*

I was never that crazy about school myself, so I can identify with part of your situation. I still haven't completely figured out how that quadratic equation makes my life more manageable today. However, there is a part of your story that concerns me. It's the part about your son faking sickness to stay home. Even the least motivated teenage scholars usually enjoy the social context of school. That's where their friends are. That's where they get caught up on all the news that's going on in each other's complicated lives. It's where they connect with their world.

Your son's behavior indicates that something else may be wrong. It would be tough to speculate on what that might be, but here are some possibilities you may want to consider. Is there a relational problem with a teacher or with some other students? Humiliating public put-downs, bullying that makes school a dangerous place, social rejection or a feeling of academic failure can drain motivation in no time. The transition into high school can also be traumatic for some students— and because he's a fifteen-year-old boy he won't want to appear weak or pathetic. Is there a learning disability that may just now be showing up and making it tough for him to keep up? On the other hand, he may be bored because he's not being challenged.

Try to determine if this has happened gradually or more suddenly as a reaction to a recent or current situation. It will be important for you to discover what is beneath your son's disdain for school. Talk to his teachers or a guidance counselor who can find out what might be going on.

In some cases what you are describing may be an indication of a deeper, more serious issue like depression, drug abuse or even some kind of physical or neurological condition. If the behavior continues, you may have to seek counseling to help your son sort things out.

Marv Penner

79. *Since my kids were little, we've always helped them with their homework. Now that they are teenagers, we think they should do it on their own. Just how much should I help our kids with their homework?*

It's okay to help kids with their homework, but there are different ways to help. Whatever the age of the children, however, parents should not do the work for them. Instead, we should act as advisors, counselors, guides and resources. With young children, parents will take a more hands-on approach, making sure the child has followed the directions and has done everything assigned. Mom or dad can also check the work and point the child in the right direction. But even at an early age, the child needs to do his or her own work and take responsibility for it.

With older kids, especially teenagers, parents should work at asking the right questions rather than giving answers. You could say, for example, "Have you considered . . . ?" "How would you answer someone who said . . . ?" "Why did you write that?" "Where did you get your information?" "How did you arrive at that conclusion?" or something similar. The goal of such questions is to help the young person think conceptually and analytically and to come up with his or her own answers.

We can also help our kids do better in school by making it easy for them to study at home. This includes providing a desk, study tools and good lighting, and enforcing "quiet hours" that everyone in the family respects. Your goal should be to help your kids develop personal discipline and good study habits that they can carry with them to the next level of their education, away from home and into life.

Dave Veerman

80. *This may sound like a strange problem, but my daughter (ninth grade) is a total overachiever. She's obsessed with her grades and spends hours every night doing (and sometimes redoing) her homework. She is absolutely devastated when she doesn't get straight A's in everything. I worry about her and wish she would get more sleep, relax more. Any suggestions?*

First of all, you don't say if this ninth-grade daughter is your firstborn child. But it wouldn't surprise me if she is. The parental folklore about firstborn and only-born children being overachievers has been substantiated in numerous studies, and for good reason. When parents go through infancy and childhood with that first child, every first step, first word, first anything takes on epic importance. Every micro-advance of growth in any realm is surrounded by awed parents and zooming video cameras. Every setback is accompanied by frenzied phone calls and reassuring doctors. With the firstborn child, every bump and scratch is life threatening. By the time parents have been through this two or three times, we become a bit more nonchalant: "Has the head been completely severed or is it still connected? Well then, he'll be fine." Kids pick up on this. Unconsciously, we train firstborn children to take success and failure very seriously.

Second, be conscious about how and when you affirm your child. For a lot of kids, the only route to parental affirmation goes through some form of achievement, be it athletic (sports), academic (school) or artistic (music, dance, etc.). While this is understandable, and appropriate to some extent, it can communicate more than we intend. We all know intuitively that it's possible to be an outstanding athlete, artist or student and still be a lousy human being. Just read the sports pages. That's why I remind parents, rather than always affirming achievement, to watch for character traits to affirm: honesty, loyalty, integrity, determination, kindness, generosity. Instead of just saying, "Jill, great job on the chemistry midterm!" watch for some trait of character that you can affirm. "Jill, forgive me, I wasn't trying to eavesdrop. But I heard you on the phone last night and apparently you were talking to someone about your friend Bianca, and I overheard you saying that you were 'uncomfortable' with the conversation; that it felt 'like gossiping' and that if your friend on the phone had a problem with Bianca, she 'should go directly to her.' And I just commented to your mom, 'I really respect that kind of loyalty and integrity.' "

Third—and this may be the greater danger in your case—when we only or primarily affirm achievement, it can communicate an "I love you if . . ." message that predicates mom's or dad's love on some level of accomplishment. Obviously that's not what we really intend to be saying. But if that's what they're hearing, then it certainly raises the stakes in matters of schoolwork, sports, etc. Our fast-paced, stress-

filled, overly competitive society puts enough pressure on our children to perform; let's not add any more to that than necessary.

Beyond that, I think it might be wise to just relax a bit. There are, after all, worse obsessions. And too, people have a way of adjusting their own thermostats in time. At some point, if your daughter gets tired of all the self-imposed heat, she may just dial down the pressure a bit. Meanwhile, if she senses your panic that she can't relax, that's not likely to help her calm down.

Duffy Robbins

81. We just discovered that our seventeen-year-old has been skipping school. We've tried punishing him, but nothing seems to work. What should we do?

First, find out why your son is skipping school. Sit down and have a talk with him, listening carefully not only to what he says but also to the hidden messages behind his words. Sometimes a teenager will say, "School is boring," when he really means "I'm failing." Ask questions without making accusations or threats. Try to be understanding and empathetic. If your son is a senior who is about to graduate, "senioritis" is a common malady. Or he may be afraid of bullies or having other relationship problems. There may be an undiagnosed learning disability. Sometimes kids ditch school simply to avoid the responsibility that comes with it. Your goal is to discern why he is truant. Where is he going? How is he getting there?

Now is the time to make sure your son understands why school is important and worth the effort, regardless of how "boring" or irrelevant it may seem to him. Talk about his plans for the future, his career goals. For most careers, a high school diploma, if not a college degree, is required. He needs to know that education is a very serious matter and his primary "occupation" as a teenager. The goal is not

necessarily learning the subjects that are taught, but learning to be responsible and self-disciplined. These are skills that every job requires. On the other hand, you may discover that your son is simply not student material. At seventeen years old, he may need to take a break from school and get a job to give him time to decide what kind of education he wants to pursue.

The next step is to contact the school and work with teachers and faculty to arrive at a workable solution. Request a conference with his teachers to find out what is happening inside the classroom. Are there problems that teachers may be aware of? Are they willing to work with you to come up with a plan to hold your son accountable and to monitor his performance on a weekly, if not a daily, basis. You may want to draft a letter or contract that gives your son's teachers permission to call you during the day if they notice any misbehavior, lack of attentiveness, missed assignments and the like. Assure them that your son is aware of the contract you are proposing and understands the consequences of noncompliance.

Third, help your teen solve his problem. Put the ball in his court. Let him help figure out what to do. There needs to be a system of accountability that works for both your son and the school. Let him know that you will be monitoring his school attendance and performance closely (make sure you have a way of doing this). Also let him know what the consequences will be for failing to show up for class or for missing assignments. Find out what privileges, activities or personal possessions are important to your son, and make them part of the equation. "Skip school and you will be grounded one weekend day for every day of school you skip. That means no friends, no TV, no stereo, no going out, no fun." If he is using the car to ditch school, then driving privileges can be taken away.

It's obvious that you are more concerned about his school attendance

Talk to your daughter about all the issues. Communication is better than contraception. Before she continues being sexually active, she needs to decide if having sex before marriage is a wise choice.

Your daughter needs to know the real risk of sexually transmitted diseases (STDs). The probability for contracting a disease multiplies enormously for people who engage in promiscuous sex. Basically when you have sex with a person, you are having sex with everyone they've had sex with. Using the pill or a condom does not prevent being infected by a sexually transmitted disease.

And there's no foolproof way to avoid a pregnancy. Your daughter needs to know that if she becomes pregnant she'll have four choices, all very difficult.

- Raise the baby herself. Eighty percent of mothers who do this end up living in poverty for the rest of their lives.

- Put the baby up for adoption—and spend a lifetime wondering what's happening with your child. Yet, last year 2 million loving family adoption requests were unfulfilled.

- Have an abortion. I hope and pray this doesn't happen both for moral and psychological reasons.

- Get married to the boy. Having to get married is never a good way to start. If the boy doesn't want to get married, he is still legally and financially responsible for his child all the way through college.

Remember that it's never in our children's best interests to rescue them from consequences, but rather, to make sure they understand that they have the power to make wise choices and to determine the kind of life they want to live. Providing birth control pills is not the best way to teach responsibility to your daughter. She needs to learn responsibility on her own.

Jim Green

and go to jail?" or, "My teenager insists on playing on the busy free-way. He says it's real exciting. Should I buy him a helmet in case he gets hit by a speeding car or truck?"

If you believe that sex before marriage is wrong (and I hope you do), then talk with your daughter about that. This is the time for her to hear you say, "Darling, I cannot help you do something that will affect the rest of your life. I want you to be happy. I want you to enjoy sex for all of your life, not just now. The best way for that to happen is for you to someday be in a committed arrangement called marriage." You can either let your daughter know where you stand and what you believe is right, or you can sit by and let her continue in a path that is immoral, unhealthy, irresponsible, always risky and often the road to disease and unhappiness.

Do whatever it takes to protect her. This will not happen by putting locks on her bedroom door. It means building a new relationship built on openness, affection and, at times, tough love, sticking to your abstinence guns.

This may be the time to examine why your daughter feels a need to have sex with her boyfriend. A lot of sexually active teenagers come from homes where there isn't much affection, where parents are too busy with their own lives to provide that. Many teen girls get involved sexually with boys because they are seeking intimacy. They have a desire to be held, to be loved, to be desired. Very few girls seek sex for the sake of having sex. That's why fathers especially need to express love to their daughters by being involved in their lives and being appropriately affectionate. Your daughter needs to feel cherished and adored by dad.

Some teens use sex as a form of rebellion. Maybe they want to get back at their parents by getting pregnant or by saying, "If you don't care about me, I'll find someone who cares."

36. We found pornography in our fifteen-year-old son's bedroom. We aren't sure how to handle this situation. For one thing, we know he'll be angry when he discovers that we were snooping around in his things. Any suggestions?

You raise two issues: pornography and privacy. Let's take the pornography issue first. It should come as no surprise to you that at age fifteen, your son has become a sexual being. God created us that way. There is heightened curiosity about sex from the time we enter middle school (or for some, earlier!). One of the ways young men in particu-

PORNOGRAPHY IS EVERYWHERE

One of my professors told his class about the time his middle-school son had a Playboy magazine hiding in his room. Somehow, the magazine was discovered. The boy was embarrassed, but Dan (the dad) said, "Let's discuss what is being portrayed here." Dan said, "I never want you to feel that you cannot talk about this stuff with me." This opened a door for Dan and his son to discuss sexual issues such as dating, abstinence, purity, "how far is too far" and how to handle lust.

Pornography is everywhere. There were 260 million pages of porn online, an increase of 1800 percent since 1998. Porn amounts to about 7 percent of the 3.3 billion pages indexed by Google. Boys tend to be tempted by this more than girls. Recent studies suggest a correlation between heightened aggressiveness in boys and exposure to pornography. Some studies state that young boys stimulated by pornography may become sexual abusers in adulthood.

My former professor was breaking the sexual code of "silence" by talking about it! Joshua Harris's Not Even a Hint (Multnomah) is an easy-to-read, practical and biblical book for young people on guarding against lust. For those with a son, I would encourage you to read with him Preparing Your Son for Every Man's Battle by Stephen Arterburn and Fred Stoeker (WaterBrook Press). They point out that attraction to the opposite sex is natural, that sex within marriage is exhilarating, that sex is a slippery slope and that God has standards for sexual behavior. Discuss with your son the power (both positive and negative) of sexual temptation, the way in which guys are drawn into sexual seduction (the eye), and ways to protect the heart and mind. Your son needs to be encouraged to win the war, and in the words of the book, it is "every young man's battle."

David Olshine

lar satisfy their curiosity is to seek out information, often in the form of pornography. As you probably know, pornography is not difficult for them to find these days. If they can't find print or video pornography, it's available on the Internet and sometimes on prime-time TV!

The best way to deal with sexuality is to talk about it as honestly and openly as you know how. This is a great time for dad and son to talk. Consider this a teachable moment. Why not have a family night (or a dad and son time) once a week or once a month where you all discuss controversial subjects, using a question and answer approach. Sexuality is meant to be discussed in our homes, not just in the locker rooms at school. Create a safe place to discuss all the issues regarding sexuality, including pornography, homosexuality, masturbation, same-sex marriage, adultery and oral sex. Our kids have access to a lot more information than we think and certainly know a lot more than we did when we were their age!

The second issue is a teenager's right to privacy. It should also be no surprise to you that most parents have snooped in their teenagers' bedrooms. We have dealt with the issue of privacy elsewhere in this book, but suffice it to say that every parent has to determine their own ethics and policies regarding this issue. Personally, I am not in favor of snooping in a teenager's belongings unless there is some evidence of danger for your child or someone else (drugs, firearms, etc). Teenagers do need to feel that they have some private space, just as you do. But if you do believe that you have a right to enter your son's bedroom without a search warrant, make sure he understands this ahead of time, not after the fact.

If you feel you have violated your son's privacy, you may need to confess and apologize. Expect that there will be some fallout for some time, and don't get angry because your son is angry. You would be too.

But you may choose instead to say nothing about the "found" por-

right now than he is. By being firm and clear on rules and consequences, your goal is to transfer most of that concern to him. He is the one who needs to worry most about his school performance, not you.

You may need to implement other strategies. Perhaps your son needs some tutoring. Perhaps he needs a quiet place to study or a computer to help him do research. Maybe he needs to switch schools. You may want to consider homeschooling.

Don't forget to encourage your son and to praise him when he succeeds. He may not be getting the best grades, but you can praise him for anything he is doing right—even if it is just showing up for class or completing an assignment. Many teens do poorly in school because they feel like failures and have lost confidence in themselves. In most cases, their opinion of themselves is a reflection of how they are treated by their parents.

If your son only skips school occasionally and hasn't hurt his grades by doing so, you may decide to relax and save your energy for bigger, more important battles. Perfect attendance badges don't really count for much in today's world. And remember, some of the brightest and most successful adults skipped school a few times when they were kids.

David Olshine

82. We have homeschooled our children through elementary school, but our daughter who is moving up to seventh grade wants to attend the public middle school. We have grave concerns about this. We are convinced that the public school system exerts a strong worldly influence on our children, and today the middle schools and high schools are full of drugs, sex and violence. But our daughter insists that she can handle the pressures and influences of the world. We aren't so sure. Should we continue to homeschool her or let her go to the public school?

Of course, you are the ones who will have to decide, based on the school system and your daughter. To give you a specific and definite answer to your question without knowing all the facts would be rather presumptuous. As you make your decision, however, here are a few points to ponder.

First, many good reasons for homeschooling exist, but "sheltering" isn't one of them. Unfortunately, a desire to protect their kids from the evils of society is precisely what motivates many parents to keep their children home. Eventually, however, even the most sheltered children grow up, leave the shelter and have to deal with society. So whether or not they homeschool their children, responsible parents should work at helping them internalize biblical values, equipping them to become mature, responsible and contributing adults.

Second, you are right to say that schools exert a strong influence on children, but you are wrong when you imply that all our middle schools and high schools are "full of drugs, sex and violence." Certainly you can find examples of all those in most schools, just as you can in your neighborhood, but most schools also have many positive influences, not the least of whom are Christian teachers, coaches and administrators. And a whole army of youth workers want to spend time with our kids and lead them toward Christ. Check to see if Campus Life, Campus Life JV, Young Life, WyldLife, Fellowship of Christian Athletes, Student Venture and other Christian ministries are active on the campus near you. Also, work with your church youth leaders to make the youth ministry the best it can be.

Third, remember that Jesus commissioned his followers to be salt and light in the world. To effectively do that, we need to be there, in the world. Wouldn't it be great if your daughter understood her role as an ambassador for Christ on her campus? Talk with her about that and work with her to make it happen.

Fourth, know that this doesn't have to be an all-or-nothing decision. You can take it a year at a time.

In all of this, be sure to seek the counsel of other parents who have made the transition—they will have tons of good advice.

Dave Veerman

83. *Our fifteen-year-old daughter is involved in so many extracurricular activities, she no longer has time to study or attend youth group. What should we do about this?*

It is important for you and your daughter to establish the order of priority for the activities she has chosen. For our family, the priorities were simple: church and Sunday school, youth group, academics and, finally, extracurricular activities. The time commitment to the first two of those priorities was relatively easy to determine. They had set times once a week for Sunday school and church and twice a month for youth group in our case. Extra youth group activities were considered optional.

It is more difficult to determine the time commitment needed to keep academics in the third position on the list of priorities. What are your daughter's educational/vocational goals? If she is college bound, she will want to maintain a certain grade level in order to be admitted. The time she needs to meet that level of achievement will determine how much time she must commit to academics.

The next priority on the list is extracurricular activities. If there is not time for every activity she desires to participate in, she will need to prioritize this group and choose her favorites.

It is essential for parents to help their children determine priorities. Too often teenagers only consider short-term goals. A parent can help establish longer-range goals.

Kendra Smiley

84. *I have done everything I can to help my son understand the importance of getting good grades and getting accepted into a top-flight university, but he seems uninterested and unmotivated. Am I wrong to insist that he perform up to his capabilities? I'm confident that he will thank me later for keeping the pressure on him.*

Six words: If the horse is dead, dismount.

From the sound of it, you have beaten the dead horse long enough. You've "done everything," and it doesn't seem to be getting your son's attention. "Keeping the pressure on" works if you are hoping to see your son become an adult who responds best to external pressure, an adult who performs well only when his supervisor is looking over his shoulder and demanding excellence.

But my guess is that you are looking for something more. My guess is that you are hoping for your son to grow up to be internally motivated, to be someone who accomplishes his goals without someone putting pressure on him from the outside.

Start by asking yourself, *Who owns this problem?* Right now, this is clearly your problem. You are the one worried about it. You are the one carrying the stress. You are the one feeling the pressure. In fact, you are the one seeking help. (It's not likely that your son has written a letter to a teen magazine asking for help on this issue!)

Don't expect to change your son's academic apathy by taking responsibility for it yourself. A young person will rarely be motivated about education simply by his or her parents stressing how important education is. The pattern is clear: He is comfortable. You are anxious. You are motivated to change. Your son, unfortunately, is not. The secret is to find ways that your son's lack of academic motivation can become a problem for him.

You have two powerful tools for transferring "the problem" from yourself to your son. The first motivational tool you have is simply your relationship with your son. He is much more likely to come to you for counsel and advice if your relationship is intact. Be careful not to hurt your relationship over behavior that has no lasting moral significance. If you do, you may cut yourself off from having the kind of lasting influence on your son's academics that you hope to have.

Think back over your academic conversations with your son. Has he heard something that goes like this: "You did well on your history grade, but what happened with Spanish?" It may very well be that your son now assumes that he can never be good enough academically to please you, and so he has simply given up. If your relationship with him is chronically antagonistic and negative, it is not likely that he will trust your counsel, as accurate as it may be.

The second motivational tool at your disposal is consequences. They are the most effective way to let your son "own the problem" of his academic apathy, because they give teenagers clear feedback on the results of their choices, feedback that can motivate them more than words ever can. It sounds like you have already learned that pressure-laden lectures are not a very effective form of motivation. So think more consequences and fewer words.

Consequences are not random, unpredictable punishments for vague misbehavior (for example, "These grades are horrible! You're grounded for the next three weeks!"). They work when they are clearly agreed on beforehand. It is best if you and your son can agree six weeks before his grades come out what the performance expectations really are and what will happen if those expectations are not met.

Though the specifics might be different, you might use the academic consequence approach of one dad I know: "Son, I've got some good news for you. I'm not going to say a word about your grades for the next six weeks. I will not ask you about studying. I will not pressure you about grades. If at the end of the six weeks, all your grades are B or better, I will continue to let you have total control over managing your study time. But if there is even one grade below a B, you will have an involuntary study hall every weekend night for the next six weeks to insure that you will have enough time to give attention to your studies."

If you try this approach, your son will likely want to negotiate the specifics of the arrangement. You will be wise to let him win something in the negotiation, since negotiation is a much more valuable skill in adulthood than arguing. The key at this point is not that you get your way but that the two of you agree on an objective consequence for academic underperformance.

The six weeks of academic freedom may motivate your son, but don't count on it. He may need the harder motivation of studying on weekend nights to fully accept that now he really does "have a problem."

Mark DeVries

VALUES AND FAITH

85. *We have had family devotions with our children since they were little. Now that they are teenagers, they no longer want to participate. We are considering ending this important family tradition rather than allowing it to become a source of arguing and boredom for our kids. What do you think?*

Family devotions are a great idea. But they must adapt as the children in the family grow and mature. It is highly unlikely that what was effective with your children in their preschool days or even during elementary school will be the pattern you will want to use in the teenage years. It is important to ask yourself the question *What is the goal of our family devotions?* For us, we wanted to take some time each day to share God's Word with our kids and make application of the Word. We never demanded complete silence or uninterrupted attention. In fact, I have fondly referred to our time of family devotions as "devotion commotion." Nevertheless, we met our main goal each morning.

After you have determined your goal, you can probably adapt your former style of family devotions to accommodate the changing dynamics of your family. Why are they arguing and bored? Eliminate the elements that cause the negative reactions and use a little creativity to modify your original plan. Remember, teenagers tend to prefer shorter and more direct teaching. It is not the length of time spent in family devotions that matters.

Kendra Smiley

86. Our teenager absolutely refuses to go to church. Is this a battle worth fighting with him? What should we do?

God's Word is pretty clear about how important it is to set aside a time of worship. The line "I can worship God at home. Why do I have to go to church?" is overused. And the reply that always comes to my mind is, "Do you worship God at home?" Chances are the answer is no.

In our home, going to church was something we all did, every Sunday morning. That meant we didn't just expect the kids to go, but the adults were always in church too. For us, worship was a required element of the week. Because it was never an optional item, it was not an arguable point with our kids, even in the teenage years.

Could it be that your church is not teen friendly? Should you look for one that is? A good youth program is also essential. If your child knows of a youth program that is vibrant and exciting, I would encourage you to check into the church that sponsors that program.

Is your teenager's disinterest in attending church actually an act of defiance against you? Then there is really no debate. You are the parent and you can require attendance in church each Sunday. If that is a rule of your household, enforce it. But perhaps you could be flexible enough to allow your teenager to have some choice in the church he attends. Perhaps by attending another church, he will have less need to "rebel" in harmful ways. Many parents have found this to be a very successful way to encourage church attendance without forcing their teenager to go with them.

Kendra Smiley

87. *How in the world can parents compete with the glamour and glitz of the entertainment media and the power of the peer group? I want my kids to grow up with a sense of right and wrong, what's true and what's false, but I feel like a voice crying in the wilderness. They don't listen to me. They listen to their friends and all the celebrities who look cool. Parents are not cool.*

Can parents compete with the glamour and glitz of the entertainment industry and the power of the peer group? Perhaps a better question is, "Can the entertainment industry and the peer group compete with the influence of parents?"

No contest. The results of that competition are already in, and parents win in a landslide. Think about it. How many adults look back on their adolescent years and credit the entertainment industry or their buddies at school with having the most enduring influence in their lives? The answer is very few. And my guess is that for those who *do* give the nod to the entertainment industry or their peers, their parents probably weren't in the game at all. They forfeited, and the entertainment industry and peer group scored a TKO by default.

> **HAPPY KIDS**
>
> *I have worked with teenagers for many years, and you'd think that the happiest teens would be those who can do everything they want, go where they want, come in when they want, etc. But I've found that not to be true. Most of these teens are not happy; they usually feel lonely and do not feel their life really matters. Strangely, the happiest teens are those with boundaries, rules and standards, with parents who lovingly enforce those standards.*
> *Jim Green*

Decades of research on this topic is consistently conclusive. The entertainment industry and the peer group can't hold a candle to the influence of caring, involved adults, especially parents, in the life of a teenager. You may feel like a voice crying in the wilderness from time to time, but don't stop being that voice. It's still early in the game, and by the time your kids reach adulthood, those celebrities and friends will be a distant memory. Almost without exception, teenagers return to the tracks that were laid for them by their parents. They may get derailed for a while, but sooner or later the light comes on and they realize that even though mom and dad weren't very cool, they were correct.

Here are some things you can do to stay in the game:

- Don't stop teaching them what you believe. The Bible instructs parents to teach their children "when you sit at home and when you walk along the road, when you lie down and when you get up" (Deuteronomy 6:7). Don't give up because your teenager doesn't seem to be listening. They are listening more than you think.

- Be clear about your standards. Provide rules and limits that are consistent with your values, and enforce them consistently.

- Live out your values and faith in front of your kids. There is no more powerful way to teach than by modeling. When kids become teenagers, they listen less but they watch more. They will learn best by your example.

- Make church attendance mandatory for everyone in your family. Support your church's youth ministry and encourage your kids to get involved. If your church doesn't have a youth ministry, find one that does or allow your kids to attend a youth group of their choice.

- Be patient. The Bible says, "Train a child in the way he should go / and when he is old he will not turn from it" (Proverbs 22:6). While there are no guarantees, this is an encouragement to parents to not give up and to trust that the game isn't over until it's over. When Jesus wanted to describe God the Father, he chose a story of a father whose rebellious son ran away from home (Luke 15). Many parents can identify with that father and the pain he was going through as he waited for the son to come home. But like most wayward children, his son eventually returned.

Remember, you don't have to be "cool." Just be a plain old uncool parent who provides your kids with the love and guidance their favorite celebrities and peers have no clue about. One of these days your kids will thank you big time.

Wayne Rice

88. *Our seventeen-year-old daughter believes that she is a witch. Seriously, she has joined a group at school that promotes the Wicca religion, which I understand is the practice of witchcraft. Is this just a phase she's going through, or should we be concerned?*

Yes, you should be concerned. Wicca is an ancient religious cult that is rising in popularity with young people. If your daughter is immersing herself in Wicca, you should be informed about a few of its practices and beliefs. In summary:

- Wicca involves meditation, chanting, music, dance, visualization and ritual drama. Its primary life principle is, Do nothing to harm yourself or others. Sounds pretty harmless so far.

- But Wiccans reject the Judeo-Christian God of the Bible and Jesus Christ as Savior. Instead, they teach that there is a "goddess" who dwells within each person. The goal is to get in touch with this goddess, the universal mother, source of fertility and wisdom. They also deny the existence of Satan, but they do affirm the existence of "evil spirits" and the "dark side." They also believe in reincarnation.

- Wicca borrows from storybook witchcraft in that it incorporates brooms, wands, cauldrons, crystals, pentacles, books of magic (containing incantations, spells, rituals and magic) and bells to ward off evil spells and spirits.

■ Wicca is a cult that blends Hinduism, Buddhism, eastern mysticism, magic, witchcraft and shamanism.

What to do?

First, don't let this destroy the relationship you have with your daughter. Keep the communication lines open.

Second, stay calm. No doubt your daughter told you she was a witch just to see what kind of reaction she would get from you. The more angry or critical of her you become, the more she will harden her position and break off communication. Sometimes kids try shocking their parents as a way to gain their independence. If it doesn't work, they try something else.

Third, do your homework. Learn all you can about Wicca. There are lots of books and websites that can provide you with the facts about it. The more you know, the more you will be able to talk intelligently to your daughter about it. There's a good chance she doesn't even realize what she's getting herself into.

Fourth, set limits where you can. You can't force your daughter to believe or not believe anything, but you can enforce curfew rules, car privileges and so forth. If her practice of Wicca is adversely affecting her school or family life, you can disallow her participation in it on that basis. You can also enforce any rules you have regarding church attendance. If she continues to be exposed to the truth, it will set her free.

Fifth, pray daily for her. There's a good chance this is just a fad that will pass like all the others, but maybe not. Your daughter is in real danger. Pray and trust that God is more powerful than any pagan religion. He is capable of delivering her from this.

David Olshine

89. We have tried to encourage our teenager to get involved with the youth group at church, but he refuses. He thinks the other kids who attend are losers. Should I force him to go?

My quick response is yes, but I don't know your son or the youth ministry. This reaction is not unusual—many teenagers from the best youth groups ever say that the groups are "stupid, dumb and boring." So don't be alarmed. "Force," however, doesn't mean a knock-down-drag-out argument. Just let your teenager know, calmly and quietly, that attendance at the youth group is mandatory. This shouldn't be a fight. Then, at another time and away from home, try to have a rational discussion with him about church. Explain your reasons and listen to his. Ask him to describe what a good youth ministry looks like and why he thinks the other kids are "losers."

Also, work behind the scenes with your youth worker. Share how your son feels, and enlist his or her help and support. Encourage the youth worker to build a friendship with your son and to include him in activities with kids he would enjoy. The youth worker doesn't ever have to tell your son about the conversation; it's private, between the two of you. Hopefully, the two of you can be allies in ministering to your son. In this conversation, brainstorm with the youth worker about how to make the youth ministry great and what you can do to help make that happen.

In extreme cases (the youth group really is terrible and so is the youth director), you should allow your son to find another youth group. Don't allow him to use the situation at your church as an excuse to skip church altogether.

Dave Veerman

90. How can I teach my son to be more considerate of others and less *self-centered? It seems like all he cares about is himself. Are all teenagers this way?*

Unfortunately, most teenagers are wired with a predisposition to being pretty self-absorbed. Certainly there are exceptions, but your son is not alone in his apparent imbalance. When we understand what is causing it, maybe we won't take it quite as personally. Part of it is egoism, part of it is relational immaturity, and part of it is just plain fear. Sometimes self-centeredness can look like cocky overconfidence, but for most kids it's more about relational insecurity and lack of self-assurance.

Here's what's going on: as kids get into their early teens they begin to detach from family. It's good and right that they do this. (We don't want them living at home forever!) The problem is that as they disconnect from us to begin forming their own separate identity they can begin to feel very vulnerable and unprotected. It seems to them that their only choice is to protect themselves. Looking out for number one is a means of survival in what feels to many kids like a big scary world.

Does that mean we simply call it a phase and try to ignore it? Of course not. Just because there's a reason, it doesn't mean there's an excuse. These are the years when habits and patterns are being formed. A wise parent will recognize this as an opportunity to address unhealthy attitudes and challenge them before they become entrenched as an adult way of life.

Let me suggest that instead of merely reprimanding the inappropriate choices, you look at some of the issues that may be behind them. The first (and perhaps toughest) step in the process is to do a quick self-assessment. First, ask yourself, *To what extent is my son simply replicating some of the self-serving attitudes he sees in me?* And second, *What have I done up to this point in his life to reinforce this notion that the world revolves around him?* Sometimes the way we serve our kids creates the notion for them that the world owes them everything. We can actually handicap them by making life too easy for them.

Another proactive thing we can do is to create opportunities for service. Adopt a Third World kid through an organization like Compassion International. Take on a service project as a family. Help out at the food bank for an afternoon, organize a family missions trip or volunteer as a family at the local day camp.

The important thing to remember is that many of the attitudes our kids adopt are learned by watching us. Model service and selflessness; affirm expressions of consideration for others as you observe them in him, and find ways to provide safety and security in your home so that the survival instinct won't need to be so strong.

Marv Penner

91. *I get frustrated trying to pass my values and beliefs on to my teenagers. As their father, I get the feeling they just aren't paying attention anymore. Aren't teens in kind of a "been there, done that" mentality with dads and only open to the influence of someone new?*

A recent Gallup survey reported that seven out of ten teens would like to spend more time with their fathers. Most teens are open to having more time with dad; but they are also open to others who might mentor them as well. Eighty-five percent of the teens in the survey said that they would like a mentor in their life. So the stale image of the "generation gap" doesn't apply to today's teens. They are open to having a relationship with adults and are interested in more time with dad. This shouldn't surprise us, because half of these teens are children of divorce.

Studies have consistently shown that the more actively involved a father is with the raising of his children, the more successful those children are likely to become—academically, emotionally and socially. There is no time during a child's development when dad is dispensable; but the middle school years are the most crucial of all. It is often at this point when the father backs off from his involvement, from expressing affection, from playing with his child and seeking to make a connection. This is a mistake, because this is when your child needs it the most.

It is at this vulnerable stage when a daughter is seeking acceptance and validation from a male; if she receives it from her father, it will meet her needs of approval and reaffirm that she is valuable in her father's eyes. If she doesn't receive her father's validation, she is likely to seek it in less appropriate ways in the arms of a boyfriend.

Your role as the father of teenagers needs to be one that is less of a director and more of a coach/consultant. This allows the teenagers to assume responsibility for their own behavior but still allows you to influence them without micromanaging them. It also allows you to mentor your teen on what matters most.

Tim Smith

MONEY

92. *How long should I give my teenager an allowance? How much is appropriate?*

An allowance should serve two purposes. First, it should give your teen a chance to learn something about discretionary spending— "How will I use the resources that I have?" Second, it should allow your child some opportunity to learn the discipline of budgeting— "How can I set aside some of my short-term resources in pursuit of long-term goals?" Like any other skill, these lessons are learned through opportunity, practice, and trial and error. If the allowance is nonexistent or too low for the child's needs, they won't learn lesson number one. If the allowance is excessive for the child's needs, they won't learn lesson number two.

Taking into consideration the fact that children will vary in their discovery and grasp of these principles, you want to create a situation in which these two skills are learned. With that in mind, the proper amount of allowance should be calculated as a function of two counterbalancing variables:

1. The child's needs. As our children grow older, we can shift over to them some of the responsibilities for their own personal care. Obviously, the more responsibility we allow them to own, the more allowance we must be prepared to provide. The allowance for a five-year-old who really doesn't need money is going to be quite different from the allowance of a high school student who is responsible for her own cosmetics and toiletries.

2. *The child's ability to earn money.* As our children grow older, they have greater earning potential. It may be that their earning potential is diminished for one good reason or another (education, mission work, etc.), and we may wish to continue providing supplemental income so that they can pursue these goals. But any financial help at this point should be more of a supplement than an allowance.

In short, we will want to set an allowance that is large enough to meet the need, but not so large that it shrinks the need to earn and budget.

Duffy Robbins

93. *My teenager thinks he should be paid for doing household chores. We think the roof over his head and the food on the table should be pay enough. Who's right?*

You both are. There are some things that every family member should do to contribute to the smooth functioning of the home. There are other chores that can be assigned to your son with some "salary" attached to them.

Did you know that most families require twenty-five hours of work each week just to keep going? Make a list of what each family member does and how much time it takes just to keep the family fed, clothed, clean and in their right minds. Your son probably doesn't think about the hours you shop, pay the bills, wash his clothes, organize and schedule for the family. As a family, discuss the list and ask if you are forgetting anything. Volunteer to take the jobs you have to (like paying the bills) and ask, "Who wants to take grocery shopping for the month?" "Who wants to be in charge of yard work?" etc.

Remind your kids that families have members, not guests, and that each team member must do his or her part to keep the family working. Let them know that each family member is expected to contribute some chores because he or she is a member but that they will be paid for other chores. Make sure that you refer to this as their "salary," not their allowance. If they don't do the work, they don't get the full pay.

I meet many parents who have done a good job of sharing their standard of living with their teens but a lousy job of training them with the skills they will need to achieve that standard on their own. As a result, too many teens have a sense of entitlement—believing that it's someone else's job to take care of their needs or wants.

Sometimes giving our kids too much is giving them too little. Help your teen learn how to prepare for life by becoming "response-able"—able to respond to life's situations. Remember the parenting paradox: the more parents seek to make their teen happy, the more likely that the teen will someday be miserable. The goal here isn't a happy teen but a competent one.

Tim Smith

94. What are some things I can do to teach my teenager the value of a dollar? He seems to think that money grows on trees.

There are several things you can do to teach your teenager financial responsibility. First, and probably most important, you can model it. In today's world it is common practice to spend not only all we earn but also much more. It is the norm to spend what will potentially be earned. Rather than operate in that popular way, it is much more prudent to model delayed gratification. If your teenager observes you making wise choices about expenditures and waiting to purchase certain items until you can afford the item itself (and not just the payments), you will be a good example for him.

Another thing you can do is to tithe your income and encourage your teenager to do the same. The sooner a child gets into the habit of giving 10 percent of their "income" to Christian service, the sooner that scriptural direction becomes a good financial habit. Tithing $0.10 when he has earned $1.00 is a great way to start. Then when your teen's earning power increases, he will be comfortable giving 10 percent, and it won't be too difficult for him.

And finally, it is important for you to model saving a portion of your income. Putting a portion of the money you have earned into savings will persuade your teen to do the same. And because of the principal of compound interest, it is a very wise financial decision.

Kendra Smiley

95. Our son wants to get a job so that he can have extra money to spend. We worry that a job will only interfere with his schoolwork and other responsibilities. What do you think?

It is possible that a job will interfere with your son's schoolwork, and it is possible that it will not. It is up to you to be certain that it does not. If the initial examination of the proposed job seems to be feasible, then let your son give it a try. If he does not shirk his responsibilities at home or at school, then it would seem he is able to balance his life with the addition of the job. If he falls behind in any of his other responsibilities, then adjustments will have to be made. The adjustments might be reduced hours on the job or quitting the job completely. Help your son evaluate the situation.

Kendra Smiley

THE DOWNSIDE TO WORK

When young people are working during the school year, extracurricular activities such as sports, musical groups, plays and the like are the first thing to be squeezed out. Most of these activities require attendance at practices, games, meetings and performances after school or in the evening, which is the only time teens have left after attending classes and getting some sleep. Even if the actual hours do not conflict, most working teens will still avoid extracurricular activities because of the overall pressure on their time. They would rather fill up their off hours with socializing, shopping and perhaps even studying.

Speaking of studying, that's the next activity to be eliminated from the working student's life. School becomes less of a priority for them. A high school principal told me that a student had requested a reduced school schedule, less than the legal requirement, so she could put more hours into her job. When the principal asked why she needed to work, the girl explained that she wanted to buy a car.

Young people who neglect classes, homework and extracurricular activities cheat themselves out of a great experience and limit their future. Instead of laying a solid educational foundation for a wide variety of career options in the future, they limit themselves to dead-end jobs that give them wanted cash today.

Working teenagers also curtail their involvement in church and youth group activities. Many jobs require that they work on Sundays, so they sacrifice worship and other spiritual input.

In some extreme cases the demands of a job become so great that teenagers are left with very little time for family and friends. For whatever reason, some kids fill up every available hour with work, stopping off at home only to sleep, change clothes and grab a bite to eat before heading off to school or their job.

Because work can pull teenagers away from school, church, family and friends, I recommend not allowing your teenager to work during the school year. If they have to work to help support themselves or the family, keep the working hours minimal, and make studies and extracurricular activities important.

If your teenagers want to work during their school vacation weeks and during the summer months, that's a different matter. With no conflicts from school, your teenager can be encouraged to work as much as possible, saving money for the future and also learning some work-related skills.

Dave Veerman

96. *Should teenagers have their own credit cards? What about bank accounts? We'd like for our son to become financially responsible, but we're afraid he'll just run up a lot of credit card bills and bank fees that he (and we) can't afford.*

I visited with an exhausted college student recently who was working two jobs in addition to being a full-time student. When I asked why she was working so much, she admitted tearfully that she had run up a $6,000 credit card bill over the past semester and now was faced with the overwhelming task of paying off that bill while she was still in school. She grew up in a home where her spending was so closely controlled that she was simply never given the opportunity to make mistakes with money. And so her first financial mistakes were costly indeed.

When our kids were as young as third grade (when they were just learning what a signature was), we got them checking accounts. We wanted them to be able to experience buying their own monthly meal ticket for school and giving their own money to church.

There is something about the intentionality of sitting down to write a $1.00 check to charity that helped our kids see themselves at a very young age as givers. They learned that there is a place for spontaneous charity (like putting money into the Salvation Army bucket at Christmastime). But we wanted our kids to learn the lifetime habit of giving a percentage of their income. And when they had to slow down to calculate how much of the $20 they earned lawn mowing or baby-sitting would be given away, they couldn't help but see sharing and giving as a core part of their identity.

As you decide how you will instill financial responsibility in your children, you'll want to remember a few key principles:

- The best time to make your first money mistakes is when the stakes are small. A teenager who blows his entire month's allowance in two hours at a carnival booth will likely be more cautious after enduring twenty-plus days with no discretionary income. This is a perfect opportunity to let the consequence do the work for you. Don't waste a perfectly good consequence by piling a lecture on top of it.

- The lower the age, the more frequent the income. Children ages twelve and younger tend to do best with a weekly allowance and a weekly ten-minute meeting to allocate the allowance to giving, saving and spending accounts. With teenagers, a monthly allowance can give them the challenging experience of making their money last for an entire month.

- Because young people are, well, young, they will need a safety net to protect them against falling too far into financial problems. This is where your banker can be of great help to you. He can introduce you to "credit cards" that are preloaded to a specified amount or checking accounts that require your co-signature. These products can help give your son the freedom to make a few mistakes but also insure a limit to how big his mistakes can be.

Particularly as our kids begin to drive, it is wise for them always to have an emergency "credit card" with a low spending limit that can allow them to get gas or get help in the case of an emergency. But here too, make sure the card is in your name, since most credit cards will be only too happy to offer your son or daughter an increased spending limit without your even knowing it.

Mark DeVries

14

NONTRADITIONAL
FAMILIES

97. *I have heard about how important it is for parents to stay married and to provide children with a stable home life. In the years following my divorce, I have learned firsthand how true that is. But now I am considering remarriage, and it's very difficult to be as confident about this as I was when I was married to my children's father. I also know that 87 percent of second/third marriages fail over how to handle children from a previous marriage. This is so scary to me! I believe that it is my responsibility to put my spouse before my children, and vice versa. But my boyfriend has told me that he will never put me before his biological children. I'm afraid to get into a situation like this, afraid of another failed marriage. Do you have any insight on second marriages and this issue?*

It is true that a strong and stable marriage provides the best environment for raising happy, healthy, self-reliant children. It's hard to argue with that fact of life. Children always do better when their parents stay together and model a loving relationship in front of them. Is this principle still true in a blended family? The answer is yes, but it may have to be applied differently.

Your boyfriend sounds like a good father to his children. They need assurance that they will not lose their father's love because he has chosen to remarry. The issue for both of you is no longer "who do I put first, my spouse or my children?" but rather "how do I assure my children now that there is stability and security and enough love for everybody in our home?" Even in a blended family, it's important for children to have a solid, loving, healthy marriage modeled for them by their parent and stepparent. Parents need to be in agreement on parenting issues such as house rules, discipline and so forth. This takes extra effort, good communication and a lot of time, of course.

If you and your boyfriend marry, remember that your biological children were with you first, as his were with him. Just as the birth of a child should not destroy a marriage, so a second marriage should not destroy the special relationship that a parent has with his or her children. That's one of the real challenges of living in a blended family—establishing the new family as an important foundational reality in the lives of children without negatively affecting their identities as children of their biological parents.

Only you can decide whether you are marrying someone who will be able to provide you with the love and commitment that is required of a marriage and also remain a good father to his children. If you marry, anticipate that his children will become a very important part of your life as your children will become a part of his. You can still celebrate and nurture your new marriage while respecting and protecting the bond between your husband and his children. Children need to see that this is not only possible but the best thing for everyone in the family.

Wayne Rice

98. *Both my wife and I have children from previous marriages, and we recently formed a new blended family. The problem is that my wife's teenaged children don't respect my authority. What should I do?*

This can be a very sticky situation and may never be resolved amicably. Accepting a new "dad" can be difficult, regardless of the relationship with the old one. Think how you would react in a similar situation.

Perhaps the most important action you can take is to work on your relationships with the new teenagers in your life one on one. Go out for a meal or an activity and during the course of your time together, share how you feel. Explain that you understand that it must be tough to have a new "father" at this time of life; and just imagine what it must be like to suddenly have new teenage "children"—that's what you are experiencing. Be as open and honest as possible. And listen carefully without reacting or making judgments. You also need to make it clear that you are in charge, that you have parental authority, and that you and their mother are in agreement, working together. At times you will have to make decisions that won't be popular, and will even be resented. But that's okay—you're a big boy and can take it. A vote will not be taken; the family is not a democracy. But you want to be open to the teenagers' thoughts, ideas and feelings.

At home, choose your battles carefully. Resist the temptation to be drawn into a petty squabble over something of little significance. Then, when you do have to lay down the law or make an unpopular decision, do it firmly and quietly, explaining the consequences of misbehavior.

Dave Veerman

99. We are going through a divorce right now, and our teenager is very angry with us. What can we do to help her deal with the pain of her family breaking up?

Your daughter's anger is real and is based in reality. You and your spouse, for whatever reason, are breaking up the family. So let her vent and tell you how she really feels. But let her know that the divorce is not her fault. Many children of divorce believe that mom and dad wouldn't be divorcing if only they had been better or hadn't done this or that. Also, assure your daughter of your love—that you will always be her parent and always love her.

You also need to enlist the help of others who can guide your daughter through this tough time. She is experiencing a lot of pain right now. Talk with the youth worker at church or your daughter's Campus Life or Young Life leader. They work hard at building relationships and coming alongside hurting teenagers. Eventually you may want to involve a professional counselor, depending on the severity of the pain and your daughter's reaction to it.

Dave Veerman

100. *My husband and I recently divorced, and we have shared custody of our kids who are now teenagers. The problem is that we don't agree on what rules should be in place. When my children stay with me, they say I'm being too strict because their dad doesn't have the same rules. I'm not sure what to do. I feel like I'm being manipulated by my kids. Any suggestions?*

Just to put this in perspective, let's remember that kids often play their parents against each other, even when their mom and dad are happily married and living under the same roof. You don't need any more guilt for what is already a difficult situation. The first thing to do is to check with your ex-husband and make sure you are getting the truth on what is really happening. The kids may simply be trying to make the most of the situation. Also keep in mind that weekend standards might be different than those on a weekday (assuming that's how custody is split). If you discover that there is in fact a significant difference in the expected standards between your house and his, it becomes an important issue that needs to be addressed.

Just remember that whether married or divorced, when we base our parenting decisions on the whims and wishes of our kids it is always dangerous. Teens respond best to a consistent and principled approach to family life where the standards are rooted in genuine care and are applied with love and appropriate flexibility. When kids know they are loved they actually appreciate knowing what the boundaries are and what the consequences will be if the lines are crossed.

Of course, the thing that complicates this situation is that both you and your husband genuinely want your kids to enjoy being with you. The fear is that they will choose the more lenient parent over the stricter one. The good news, however, is that your relationship with them is not only based on how they experience the rules and standards at your house. It is also about your relationship with them, the daily investment you make in their lives, your commitment to knowing and caring for them, and the belief that you truly love them. Offer them a relationship and your standards will be far easier for them to handle.

Avoid the temptation to get into a rapport competition with your ex-husband. I understand how huge the stakes feel right now, but because your divorce is recent everyone is still learning how to make this work. Give it a little time. Don't put down their dad even though it seems so obvious that his parental "incompetence" needs to be exposed. There will be a tendency to try to balance the lenience you see at your ex's house with an even stricter regimen at your house. Obviously this will create a chaotic environment where the kids become nothing more than pawns in the ongoing game between you and your ex. Look at the rules your kids are balking at and ask yourself if they are rooted in love or fear.

The important thing is to be sure that your parenting is being shaped by your own convictions and your care for your children rather than a constant dance of trying to react to what's happening at dad's house. When most of your energy is being used to manage the relationship with their dad, there won't be much left for them.

Finally, if you feel that your teens are genuinely in jeopardy when they are with their dad, you might want to revisit the custody arrangements for the sake of their safety—but be really careful about this. They deserve the voice of a dad in their lives—even though that voice may not always match yours.

Marv Penner

101. *I am a grandmother raising two teenaged granddaughters and really need some pointers. We are Christians, so we have always gone to church. But lately the girls have been wanting to go the way of the world. They think church is boring, and they don't want to spend any time with the other children who attend church. I don't want to turn them away from church by forcing them to go or always putting down what they say. Could you give me some advice?*

Well, it would be nice if there were some snappy answer to your question, like locking them in a room for three days with nothing but a DVD player and a set of Veggie Tales. But in the real world our kids sometimes have their own ideas, and those ideas are that church is a drag. The fact is we can't always do much about that. But what follows are some simple suggestions that may help.

- First, talk with your church's youth pastor to see if he or she is aware of any relational breakdowns at youth group that may make it less attractive to your girls. Ask questions and avoid making demands. More often than not, the youth pastor will have some ideas for you and also commit to helping where he or she can.

- See if your granddaughters might be more willing to attend another youth group at another church. Call around to some of the other churches around town and see if you can find another church that might have a group more attractive to your granddaughters. I would suggest thinking in terms of a group that will have kids attending who also go to their high school. That might make it a little more attractive.

- See if there are service times that fit better with a teenager's schedule. You didn't say when you attend on Sunday morning, but maybe a Sunday afternoon or Saturday night service would work better. Lots of congregations are moving to more nontraditional times to accommodate changing schedules.

- If you can't get them to enter through the front door, be willing to let them enter through the back. Maybe the Sunday morning service is "boring" to them. Chances are you're not going to be able to change that right away, and, well, maybe they're right—it is boring. A growing number of congregations are developing midweek services with more modern music and a different ambiance. With nontraditional names like "The Edge," "The Flood," "The Potter's House" and "The Amway Salesman's Closet," these services may not feel like "church" to you. But far better to have your granddaughters attending something called "The Flood" on Wednesday night than something called "The Bed" on Sunday morning. Perhaps in time they will develop a taste for the worship service you attend. But until then, a different slice of the loaf is better than no loaf at all.

- Do everything you can to help your granddaughters build relationships with the kids at church. Inevitably, kids are drawn to relationships. They will go where they feel they have friends. Understandably, sometimes youth group activities can get expensive, and you may ask, "What does laser tag have to do with church?" But any youth group activity that might promote and nurture relationships will be a worthy investment. Kids go where their friends are.

- Depending on their age, I would still require them to attend some sort of Christian service each week. You can simply frame it as a matter of respect for you and the rules of your house. Often I find that kids don't know what they like, and unless they are strongly encouraged to step out of their comfort zone, they simply won't try something new. Don't be so intimidated about turning them off that you don't give them a chance to be turned on.

Duffy Robbins

ABOUT THE AUTHORS

Mark DeVries is associate pastor for youth and families at First Presbyterian Church in Nashville, Tennessee. He is the author of several books, including *Family-Based Youth Ministry,* and is general editor of the *True Love Waits Bible.* He has spent more than twenty years working with youth and families, both  in the church and in organizations like Young Life. He and his wife, Susan, have three young-adult children—two daughters and a son.

Jim Green is a veteran of more than forty years of youth ministry. He has worked with youth in several churches as well as in schools and the juvenile justice system. A popular speaker at youth and family events, he was featured on two national TV specials on the family with Barbara Mandrell and the late  Johnny Cash. He and his wife, Judy, live in the Orlando, Florida, area and have three grown children and six grandchildren.

David Olshine heads the Youth Ministry Department at Columbia International University and has worked with teenagers in local churches for more than twenty years. He has authored or coauthored more than fifteen books for youth workers and parents, and he speaks at conferences for youth and families all across North America. He and his wife, Rhonda, have two children (one who still lives at home) and live in Columbia, South Carolina.

Marv Penner is chairman of the Youth and Family Ministry Department at Briercrest Seminary in Caronport, Saskatchewan, Canada. He is also the executive director of the Canadian Centre for Adolescent Research; director of "Youth Quake," Canada's premier youth ministry event; and is a licensed marriage and family counselor in private practice. He is the author of several books, including *A Youth Worker's Guide to Parent and Family Ministry*. He and his wife, Lois, have three grown children.

Wayne Rice is the founder and director of Understanding Your Teenager seminars. He is a veteran youth worker and has authored numerous books and articles on youth, youth ministry and parenting, including *Cleared for Takeoff, Read This Book or You're Grounded* and *Junior High Ministry*. He is also the cofounder of Youth Specialties, an organization that provides resources and training for youth workers. Wayne and his wife, Marci, live in Lakeside, California, and have three grown children.

Duffy Robbins has worked with teenagers for more than twenty-five years and now serves as chair of the Department of Youth Ministry at Eastern College. A popular speaker at youth gatherings all over the world, Duffy is loved by teens for his sense of humor and his insight into teen issues. He wrote a monthly  column for teenagers in Focus on the Family's *Breakaway* magazine, and he has authored numerous books, including *Youth Ministry Nuts and Bolts, The Ministry of Nurture* and *Going the Distance*. Duffy and his wife, Maggie, live in suburban Philadelphia. They have two grown daughters.

Kendra Smiley is a former schoolteacher who now heads up her own organization called Live Life Intentionally! A dynamic communicator, she speaks to audiences all over North America. She is on the state board for the Fellowship of Christian Athletes (FCA) and has written several books, including *Helping*  *Your Kids Make Good Choices* and *Aaron's Way*. She and her husband, John, have three grown sons and live in East Lynn, Illinois.

Tim Smith has served for more than a decade as pastor of family life at Calvary Community Church in Westlake Village, California. He is currently the director of Life Skills for American Families, an organization committed to encouraging families. He has authored several books for youth workers and par-  ents, including *The Seven Habits of Highly Effective Youth Workers, The Relaxed Parent* and *Seven Cries of Today's Teens*. Tim and his wife, Suzanne, live in Thousand Oaks, California, and have two grown daughters.

Dave Veerman has worked for twenty-six years with Youth for Christ in Illinois and Louisiana, and served as the national director of Campus Life. He has authored many books on youth ministry and parenting, including *Reaching Kids Before High School, From Dad with Love, Getting Your Kid to Talk* and *Parenting Passages.* He is cofounder and director of the Livingstone Corporation in Carol Stream, Illinois. He and his wife, Gail, have two grown daughters.

CAMP SPONGEBOB

by Molly Reisner and Kim Ostrow
illustrated by Heather Martinez

Ready-to-Read

Simon Spotlight/Nickelodeon

New York   London   Toronto   Sydney

Based on the TV series *SpongeBob SquarePants*® created by Stephen Hillenburg
as seen on Nickelodeon®

SIMON SPOTLIGHT
An imprint of Simon & Schuster Children's Publishing Division
1230 Avenue of the Americas, New York, New York 10020

Manufactured in the United States of America

10 9

Library of Congress Cataloging-in-Publication Data
Reisner, Molly.
Camp SpongeBob / by Molly Reisner and Kim Ostrow ; illustrated by Heather Martinez.— 1st ed.
p. cm. — (SpongeBob SquarePants ready-to-read; #5)
"Based on the TV series SpongeBob SquarePants created by Stephen Hillenburg as seen on
Nickelodeon."—T.p. verso.
Summary: When SpongeBob becomes Sandy's assistant at Bikini Bottom's first summer camp, his
enthusiasm starts to annoy the other staff.
ISBN 0-689-86593-7
[1. Camps—Fiction. 2. Interpersonal relations—Fiction.] I. Ostrow, Kim. II. Martinez, Heather, ill. III. Series:
SpongeBob SquarePants (Television program) IV. Title. V. Series.
PZ7.R27747 Cam 2004 [E]—dc22   2003017679

It was a perfect summer day
in Bikini Bottom. Sandy spent
the morning practicing her new
karate moves.
"Hiiiyaaaa! All this sunshine
makes me more energetic
than a jackrabbit after a cup
of coffee," she said.

"Hey, Sandy, where did you first
learn karate anyway?"
SpongeBob asked.
Sandy told her friend about her days
at Master Kim's Karate Camp.

". . . and I won the championship!"
Sandy finished breathlessly.
SpongeBob leaped in the air.
"Camp sounds amazing!" he shouted.
"But I never got to go."

"When I was little, my dream
was to go to camp. But every summer
my parents sent me to Grandma's.
Sometimes I would pretend she was
my counselor, but I am not sure she
was cut out for camp life,"
SpongeBob said, sighing.

"Say no more, SpongeBob,"
   said Sandy. "Let's open Bikini
   Bottom's first summer camp.
   You can be my assistant."
"I can?" asked SpongeBob.
"Yes, and we can get started
   today," said Sandy.
"I am ready!" shouted SpongeBob.

Sandy gathered Squidward and
  Patrick to tell them about the camp.
"Oh, please," Squidward said,
  moaning. "Camp is for children."
"Exactly!" shouted SpongeBob.
"It would be for all the little
  children of Bikini Bottom."

"Hmmm," Squidward thought out loud.
"Perhaps I could teach the
    kids around here a thing or two.
Everyone would look up to me."

10

"That sounds like lots of fun,"
said Patrick. "When I was at starfish
camp, we used to lie around in the sun
and sleep a lot. I could teach
everyone how to do that!"

"I will teach karate!"
declared Sandy, kicking the air.

"Now go on home and practice what you are going to teach. Let's meet back here tomorrow," said Sandy.

The next day SpongeBob woke up
in the best mood ever.
"To be a good assistant, I need
to make sure I am prepared
with good camper activities,"
he told Gary.
SpongeBob thought of making Krabby
Patties and having bubble-blowing
contests. He imagined whole days
spent jellyfishing.

15

SpongeBob ran around his house
gathering all the items he needed.
"Whistle! Check. Megaphone! Check.
Visor! Check. Clipboard?"
Gary slithered over
to SpongeBob's bed and meowed.
"Good job, Gary! Check!"

SpongeBob went over to the mirror
and raised his arms. "Camping
assistants need to be strong!"
he reminded himself
as he flexed his muscles.
"Now I am ready!"

SpongeBob ran over
to the treedome.
Sandy was chopping
wood with her bare hands.
"SpongeBob SquarePants reporting
for duty!" he said, blowing his
whistle three times.

"As a good assistant, I request permission to check on everyone to make sure they are practicing their duties."

"Go for it, SpongeBob," said Sandy.

First SpongeBob went to Patrick's
rock. He watched quietly as Patrick
practiced the art of sleeping.
Then SpongeBob blew his whistle.
Patrick jumped up.
"Just making sure you are working
   hard," explained SpongeBob.
"Now go back to sleep!"

Next SpongeBob peeked
inside Squidward's house.
"I can't hear you," sang SpongeBob.
"Practice makes perfect."

SpongeBob went back to see Sandy,
who was working on her karate moves.
"All counselors are working hard,"
reported SpongeBob.
"Now what should I do?"

"Take a load off and have some
lemonade," suggested Sandy.
"No time for lemonade,"
said SpongeBob. "As your assistant,
I am here to assist.
How can I assist?"

"Listen, little buddy," said Sandy.
"You are acting nuttier than a bag
  of walnuts at the county fair.
  This camp is supposed to be fun."
" I will make sure it is fun!
  With my assistance, this will be
  the best camp ever!" SpongeBob said,
  cheering.

"Attention, counselors, please
report to me right away,"
SpongeBob said. They all ran to him.
"Now go back to your posts and
PRACTICE! Camp opens tomorrow."

That night SpongeBob was so
excited, he could not sleep.
He decided to visit all
the counselors just to make sure
they were ready.

"Squidward," he whispered.
Squidward was fast asleep.
SpongeBob blew his whistle.
"Just making sure you are all
set for tomorrow."
"You are killing me, SpongeBob,"
said Squidward, and he went
back to sleep.

The next morning a very annoyed
Squidward and sleepy Patrick
headed over to Sandy's treedome.
"What are we going to do about
SpongeBob?" asked Squidward.
"I refuse to be ordered around
by him anymore."

"I have just the thing
for the little guy," said Sandy.

"To express our gratitude
for all your hard work, we have a
small present for you," said Sandy.
"For me?" asked SpongeBob.
SpongeBob opened the box.
Inside was a camp uniform.

"We would like you to be the very
  first camper," said Sandy.
"But don't you need me to work?"
  asked SpongeBob.
"Nope. We were all so busy preparing
  for camp that we never advertised
  for campers! You are our first
  and only camper!" exclaimed Sandy.

SpongeBob put on his uniform.
"SpongeBob SquarePants
reporting to camp!" he shouted,
running to his counselors.
"I am ready!"